The Communist Manifesto

The Communist Manifesto

Karl Marx and Friedrich Engels

With a new introduction by Jodi Dean

The Manifesto of the Communist Party was first published in February 1848. English translation by Samuel Moore in cooperation with Frederick Engels, 1888.

This edition first published 2017 by Pluto Press

www.plutobooks.com

The full text of the manifesto, along with the endnotes and prefaces to various language editions has been taken from the Marx/Engels Internet Archive (marxists.org)

Transcription/Markup: Zodiac and Brian Basgen, 1991, 2000, 2002

Proofread: Checked and corrected against the English Edition of 1888, by Andy Blunden, 2004.

British Library Cataloguing in Publication Data
A catalogue record for this book is available from the British Library

ISBN 978 0 7453 9937 9 Paperback
ISBN 978 0 7453 9939 3 Hardback
ISBN 978 1 7868 0025 1 PDF eBook
ISBN 978 1 7868 0027 5 Kindle eBook
ISBN 978 1 7868 0026 8 EPUB eBook

This book is printed on paper suitable for recycling and made from fully managed and sustained forest sources. Logging, pulping and manufacturing processes are expected to conform to the environmental standards of the country of origin.

Typeset by Stanford DTP Services, Northampton, England

Simultaneously printed in the United Kingdom and United States of America

CONTENTS

1. Introduction by Jodi Dean 1

2. Manifesto of the Communist Party 47
I Bourgeois and Proletarians 49
II Proletarians and Communists 70
III Socialist and Communist Literature 85
IV Position of the Communists in Relation to the Various Existing Opposition Parties 101

3. Appendix: Prefaces to Various Language Editions 104

4. Afterword: Introduction to the 2008 edition by David Harvey 129

1
INTRODUCTION: THE MANIFESTO OF THE COMMUNIST PARTY FOR US

Jodi Dean

An idea whose time has come again

The importance of *The Manifesto of the Communist Party* nearly 200 years after it was written is surprising. It didn't begin as a powerful statement by important people. Published in 1848, the *Manifesto* came about after a conspiratorial London group called the League of the Just contacted Karl Marx and Friedrich Engels, who had formed a network of Communist Correspondence Committees. The Central Committee of the League of the Just convinced Marx and Engels to join them in a new, more open, Communist League. The League would publish Marx's and Engels' critical communist ideas in a public statement of the League's doctrine. Marx and Engels agreed, but Marx delayed finishing the text. The Central Committee had to harass him to get the manuscript, threatening to take 'further measures' against him if he didn't deliver. Even then, the text didn't carry out the assignment: Marx produced not a manifesto specific to the League but something more, a broader statement of how communists see the world. He even changed the name, delivering not *The Communist Manifesto* but *The Manifesto of the Communist Party*, a party which didn't actually exist. In the first published version, neither the name of the group commissioning the manifesto nor those of its authors appeared on its cover. A manuscript handed in late, with no author, sponsored by no one, in the name of a non-existent party, changed the world.[1]

The event that most profoundly registers this change is the 1917 Russian Revolution. The Bolsheviks, the more militant faction of the Russian Social Democratic Labour Party (RSDLP), led a movement of workers, soldiers and peasants in overthrowing tsarism and establishing the world's first socialist workers' republic. Just as the *Manifesto* predicted, the oppressed overthrew the oppressors. The class struggle at the basis of history once again resulted in the revolutionary reconstitution of society. The working class seized political power. After the revolution, the RSDLP changed its name to the Communist Party, occupying the space opened up by the *Manifesto*. This re-issue of *The Communist Manifesto* one hundred years after this revolutionary event pushes us to occupy this space again and take the perspective of revolution.

Is this a perspective we can take now? The Soviet Union dissolved in 1991. For some, this means the time of revolution has passed. They claim that capitalism and democracy won. Capitalism and democracy, blended together and practically the same, *proved* themselves to be better, preferable, more efficient. *Communism doesn't work*, we are told, handed the end of the USSR as evidence, as if history is always and forever the endless repetition of the same. Instead of revolution, we should direct our energies toward incremental changes. We should work for capitalism with a human face. We can't change the world, but we can focus on ourselves, on the self-transformation that comes from self-work, self-love, self-care. We can even resist, carving out little moments of freedom when we spit on the burger before serving it with a smile. But, the defenders of the status quo insist, there is no need here and now for socialists, much less critical communists who 'everywhere support every revolutionary movement against the existing social and political order of things.'[2]

Don't believe it. The uprisings, demonstrations, occupations and revolts of the first decades of the twenty-first century indicate that capitalist democracy claimed victory too soon. These days the failure of the system into which capitalism and democracy have converged is clear. Dramatic increases in economic inequality have convinced millions of people across the globe of the inability of capitalism to meet basic needs for food, housing, health, clean water and education. Planetary warming, mass extinctions, sea level rise and desertification point to the capitalist system's threat to life on earth. Corporations, financial institutions and international organisations and agreements block the people from political arenas that claim to be democratic, pushing those who want to be heard onto online networks and into the streets. One hundred years since the Bolsheviks stormed the Winter Palace, political movements across the globe are taking the perspective of revolution. A new generation is returning to communism. It is an idea whose time has come again.

The communist revolutionary Nadezhda Krupskaya said that for her husband, Bolshevik leader Vladimir Lenin, 'the teachings of Marx were a guide to action'.[3] Yet more than ten years before the Russian Revolution, the head of the German Social Democratic Party, Karl Kautsky, suggested that the *Manifesto* was obsolete. Kautsky admitted that the *Manifesto*'s principles and method were correct. Yet he used those principles and method to argue that much of the *Manifesto*'s description of bourgeois society no longer applied. The political and economic conditions of Western Europe pointed to evolution not revolution. Kautsky admitted things were different in Russia. For Russian socialists, the *Manifesto* remained 'the best and most reliable guide', 'a compass upon the stormy ocean of the proletarian class struggle'.[4]

What about for us? Does it make sense to think that a text that the leading German socialist thought was outdated 60 years after its publication can provide us with a guide to action? The answer is yes – now more than ever.

Communicative capitalism

The fundamental premise of *The Communist Manifesto* is that economic production and circulation and the social organisation that follows from it are the basis of the politics and ideas characteristic of a particular epoch. From the perspective of political action, this means that those who are interested in revolutionary change have to begin with an understanding of the economy.

The *Manifesto* describes the world of nineteenth-century capitalism, what Marx refers to as the epoch of the bourgeoisie (although Engels is listed as co-author, he credited Marx for the basic ideas). Arising out of – and thereby destroying – feudal property relations, the bourgeoisie revolutionised production. 'The East-Indian and Chinese markets, the colonization of America, trade with the colonies, the increase in the means of exchange and in commodities generally, gave to commerce, to navigation, to industry an impulse never before known, and thereby, to the revolutionary element in the tottering feudal society, a rapid development.'[5] Markets grew. Rising demand and competition pushed the development of Modern Industry. Colossal productive forces were unleashed and with them a need for ceaseless expansion. The constant revolutionising of the instruments of production came to characterise the era. Past values and practices gave way before the value of exchange.

Bourgeois society is chaotic and contradictory. Modern Industry requires armies of workers who need wages to survive, a proletariat. The more developed, complex and specialised industry becomes, the more mind-numbing and repulsive the conditions of labour: the worker 'becomes an appendage of the machine'. Livelihood, even life, is made 'more and more precarious'. The enrichment of the bourgeoisie is accompanied by the pauperisation of the proletariat: the same competition that induces the capitalist to cut wages, compels the worker to accept the reduction. Overproduction generates crises such that production becomes destruction. Crises are endemic.

The *Manifesto*'s description of capitalist society is more accurate today than it was when it was written.[6] The world in the twenty-first century is entirely subsumed by capitalism. The capitalist system is global. Competition, crises and precarity condition the lives of and futures of everyone on earth. No one escapes – although some have accumulated enough capital to allow them better to weather the storm than others. As of 2016, the world's richest 62 people owned as much wealth as half the world's population combined.[7]

Unlike the time of steam engines and telegraphs, contemporary capitalism relies on global telecommunications networks. From the complex logistics that support a trade system built on the concentration of industrial production in special economic zones, to the automation and informatisation of productive processes that standardise and accelerate production while decreasing the need for human labour-power, to the high-speed networks enabling algorithmic trading, hedging and arbitrage in financial markets, to the new capacity for capital to capture the activities through which we reproduce our social lives, capitalism today has become communicative.

In communicative capitalism, capitalist productivity depends on the expropriation and exploitation of communicative processes. Communication serves capital, whether in affective forms of care for producers and consumers, the mobilisation of sharing and expression as instruments for 'human relations' in the workplace, or the contributions to ubiquitous media circuits that provide ever more data and metadata that can be stored, mined and sold. Capitalism has subsumed communication such that communication does not provide a critical outside. In the digital networks of communicative capitalism, each communicative utterance or contribution adds something to the communicative flow. Whether a post is a lie doesn't matter. Whether an article is ill-conceived is unimportant. What matters is simply that something was expressed, that a comment was made, that an image was liked and shared. Even something well-argued, true and important to a matter of real concern rarely or barely registers because the stream of contributions is endless, constant. Something else that is true and important will not just appear tomorrow but is appearing at the same time, in the same feed, making the same demands for attention. As contributions to circuits of information and affect, then, the content of our utterances is unimportant.

As the over-production of words and images intensifies and accelerates, the two merge into memes and emojis. Words are counted in word clouds, measured by number of times repeated rather than considered for what they might mean. People circulate images, unsure as to how ideas expressed in words will be interpreted or received. The decline in a capacity to transmit meaning, to symbolise beyond a limited discourse or immediate, local context, characterises communication's reconfiguration into a primarily economic form. Critique becomes indistinguishable from endorsement as the adage 'there's no such thing as bad publicity' comes to characterise all mediated interactions – at least someone was paying attention. The channels through which we communicate reward number, getting us to believe through our practices that more is better, that popularity is the standard of value. Communicative interactions thereby take on the dynamics and attributes of markets and jettison their critical capacity.

Other names for 'communicative capitalism' are information society, knowledge economy and cognitive capitalism. They designate the same formation, but each highlights something different. 'Information' points to content, although hardware, software and circulation are implied. 'Knowledge' points to combinations of content and skill (know-how and know-that). 'Cognitive' suggests a narrow range of mental operations, a new use of brain power. It is linked to the idea of 'immaterial labour', which has been criticised for ignoring physical labour, embodiment and environmental impacts. 'Communicative' underscores the relation of contemporary networked capitalism to democracy. In communicative capitalism, capitalism merges with democracy, eliminating democracy's capacity to designate a critical gap within the social field. Instead of the means by which the people collectively determine their common lives and work, the practices of free speech, criticism and discussion reinforce capitalism. Television and print blur into social media, where scandal and outrage circulate more easily than policy analyses or careful arguments. Everyday communicative exchanges – proliferating in social media – take on the same forms: memes, lists, emojis, reaction gifs and teasers.

Communicative capitalism is that capitalist system in which democratic practices and ideals of inclusion and participation merge with, enable and accelerate capitalist winner-take-all dynamics of circulation, aggregation, dispossession and accumulation. In the words of the *Manifesto*, our 'very ideas are but the outgrowth of the conditions of [our] bourgeois production and bourgeois property'.[8] Linguistic, affective and unconscious being together, flows and processes constitutive not just of being human but of broader relationality and belonging, are co-opted for capitalist production. Our basic communicative activities are enclosed in circuits as raw materials for capital accumulation. Our Facebook updates and Google searches, as well as the GPS locations signalled by our mobile phones and the steps, calories and heart rates monitored by our apps, provide data that is stored, mined and sold. Communication serves as a primary means for capitalist expropriation and exploitation.

When capitalism subsumes basic communicative activities, most of us can't avoid producing for capitalism. The concept of 'circuits of exploitation' helps explain why as it draws out the paid, precarious and unpaid labour that global communication networks link together.[9] Consider the smartphone. It is produced by factory labour, is a tool for multiple types of paid as well as precarious labour, and provides a key means through which content provided by unpaid communicative labour is generated, circulated, stored and mined. The circuit of exploitation around the smartphone links activities that take place continents apart: the extractive mining that provides the phone's raw materials, the enormous factories in which the phones are assembled, and the sleek corporate campuses where the phones are designed. Further nodes in the circuit include mobile work – work that relies on smartphones as tools for making connections and supplying content, support work – such as sales, tech-support, call centres and programming – and the work of social reproduction – communicative activities through which we build lives together with friends and family. A final node in the circuit of exploitation is e-waste, the seemingly endless mountains of outdated equipment piling up in dumps and landfills. The smartphone, then, lets us see how such radically different activities as mining, texting, sharing on social media and using apps for rides and deliveries are processes in the circuit through which capitalism intensifies competition and extracts value.

The computer scientist Jaron Lanier writes, 'We've decided not to pay most people for performing the new roles that are valuable in relation to the latest technologies. Ordinary people "share," while elite network presences generate unprecedented fortunes.'[10] Facebook illustrates Lanier's point. Facebook has over a billion active users. We make it in common, but it does not belong to us. Critics of Facebook tend to focus on issues like bullying, addiction and, more seriously, surveillance and threats to privacy. They take the form of massive social media for granted and focus on the content, the use. By ignoring the form, they neglect how social media manifests the fact that production is always production for others. Whether affect or information, production in social media is reflexive, a production of relations. In social media, the co-operation of different individuals appears as what it is, the productive force that arises out of our combined and multiplied efforts. Rather than congealed within a commodity form that renders relations between people as relations between things, the social substance manifests itself in a clear, visceral way on Twitter, Facebook, YouTube, in all massively popular social media.

The production of the social substance that we see in Facebook and Twitter is not for itself – someone else owns it. There are a billion users and one billionaire. Facebook is explicit about this. The website declares: 'Our product development philosophy centers on continuous innovation in creating products that are social by design, which means they place people and their social interactions at the core of the product experience.' Because of property relations that allow a common product to be owned by a single person (or a corporation which, in US law, is a person), producing social relations does not enable producers to procure means of life, means of subsistence. You can't eat your friends. With social media the production of social relations is for someone else, the capitalist. We are alienated from our means of socialising even as we are completely immersed in them. The more immersed we are, the more alienated insofar as there are more hits and clicks and page views to be tracked, auctioned, sold and put back to capitalist use. On social media, alienation is less a subjective experience than it is an objective process.

Communicative capitalism severs social relations from relations through which one provides and is provided food and shelter – and this is a real contradiction. Active production of social relations is not active production of food and shelter. For more and more people, active production of food and shelter is not the active production of social relations. Most people are not paid for their productive engagement in social media. It is not the way they earn money. At the same time, most of the active production of social relations does not occur through the production of food and shelter. This means that what paid labour there is in social media produces, serves or administers something else. Social media relies on a strong, even constitutive, division between communicative labour and the labour that produces food and shelter. Emphasising this division reveals how waged labour and property are fetters on communicative production and thus instruments of alienation.

Claims that everything is 'free' in the networked economy obfuscate the reality of the loss of income people need to survive. If everything is free (or close to it) then no one earns the money to pay for food and shelter. The apps and platforms of the 'sharing' or 'gig economy' have led to a collapse in wages in every sector in which they have been introduced. The livelihoods of those working in a sector become more uncertain while the owners of the platform get rich. Uber, Lyft, Airbnb, Deliveroo, Task Rabbit and other apps that coordinate rides, rentals, deliveries and odd jobs introduce or intensify competition. As Fred Turner writes, 'they've marketized ever smaller segments of time and transformed formerly private resources (such as your car) into potential sources of profit'.[11] The flexibility that the technology promises means lower wages and longer hours for workers. Proletarianised people produce information, services, relations and networks. They make more and get less, intensifying inequality with every communicative contribution and its trace.

The advances in data capture, storage and analysis that communicative capitalism affords take on the 'character of collisions between two classes' that the *Manifesto* describes. Ever more workers are proletarianised as developments in technology enable their jobs to be simplified, codified and replaced. Some examples: the development of voice recognition capacities have enabled call centres to replace people with algorithms; Google has developed driverless cars; hotels are replacing human concierges with robots. Massive amounts of data enable the automation of an array of decision-making tasks: medical diagnoses and treatment, fraud detection, legal services, ad design, purchase and placement, stock-trading. A 2014 World Economic Forum report puts it bluntly: 'the greater the role that data play in the global economy, the less the majority of individuals will be worth.'[12]

The problem of social media is the problem of capitalism – private property and ownership. Communication under communicative capitalism is a primary means of production, but it does not belong to us in common. Mass social media like Facebook and Twitter make the fact of collective production, of social power, present and undeniable such that it seems completely bizarre and contradictory that anyone could justifiably own them, or any substantial means of production at all. They are common property but not common property, public but not public, private but not private.

The intensification of inequality in communicative capitalism is not accidental. It is a property of complex networks. Complex networks are characterised by free choice, growth and preferential attachment. Examples include academic citation networks; popular blogs, websites and social media platforms; and well-known phenomena like blockbuster movies and best-selling books. As Albert-Laszlo Barabasi demonstrates, complex networks follow a power law distribution of links. The item in first place or at the top of a given network has twice as many links as the item in second place, which has more than the one in third and so on, such that there is very little difference among those at the bottom but massive differences between top and bottom. Lots of novels are written. Few are published. Fewer are sold. A very few become best sellers. Twitter is another example: it has over a billion registered users; one pop singer, Katy Perry, has over 94 million followers. Most people have 200. Popular media expresses the power law structure of complex networks with terms like the '80/20 rule', the winner-take-all or winner-take-most character of the new economy, and the 'long tail'.

Communicative capitalism stimulates the production of networks that generate power law distributions. It relies on the creation of general fields or commons characterised by free choice, growth and preferential attachment. Out of the common a 'one' emerges, the one at the top, the one with the most hits or links, the blockbuster or superstar. Capitalist exploitation consists in stimulating the production of the field in the interest of finding, and then monetising, the one. The bigger the field, the more powerful, valuable, or elite the one. Think of a competition for the best weight-loss app or best city tourism app. The contest generates a common field that will produce a winner. Commons can be generated in various ways: in comments on a post (think of reddit and the ways that readers vote posts up and down), in web articles (think Huffington Post blogs or other sites offering lots of click bait), on Twitter. The more participation, the larger the field, the greater the inequality, that is, the greater the difference between the one and the many. Expanding the field produces the one.

The generation of a common in order to produce the one contributes to the loss of opportunities for income and paid labour, as in the collapse of print journalism and academic presses. This is a primary condition of labour under communicative capitalism. Rather than having a right to the proceeds of our labour by virtue of a contract, ever more of us win or lose such that remuneration is treated like a prize. While this practice is longstanding in art, in communicative capitalism it spreads to increasing numbers of fields. Academics, writers, architects, designers and even programmers and consultants feel fortunate to get work, to get hired, to get paid. The logic of the contest structures ever more tasks and projects as competitions, which means that those doing the work are not paid unless they win. They work but only for a chance at pay. Unpaid internships further exemplify the same point: students work for free in the hope that they will win paid work in the future.

The English political philosopher Thomas Hobbes' description of merit is helpful here. In his famous *Leviathan* (chapter 14), Hobbes explains that the one who performs first in the case of a contract *merits* that which he is to receive from the performance of the other. Because the first has performed (in accordance with the contract), the second is obliged to give the first what is due him. In the instance of a prize, we also say that the winner merits his winnings, but there is a difference: the prize is the product of the event, the contest. The relation between the one awarding the prize and the winner depends on the goodwill of the giver. Nothing specifically links the winner to the prize. The implication of communicative capitalism's shift from contract to contest, from wages to prizes (the consent to which is manufactured in part via so-called reality television competitions), is the mobilisation of the many to produce the one. Without the work of the many, there would not be one (who is necessarily contingent). Many work for free so that one winner can be paid.

The administration of US President Barack Obama implemented inducement prizes through its 'Strategy for American Innovation'. Outlining a vision for a more competitive America, the White House announced that government 'should take advantage of the expertise and insight of people both inside and outside' Washington by using 'high-risk, high-reward policy tools such as prizes and challenges to solve tough problems'.[13] What went unmentioned: the characteristics of those in a position to take risks. Contests privilege those with resources insofar as they transfer the costs associated with doing work to contestants. People pay to do work for which they will not be remunerated. Work is done and then maybe paid for (the winner) and likely not (the losers).

When work is arranged as a contest, each contestant faces the uncertainty previously assumed by the capitalist and part of the justification for the capitalist's claim to profit from the value generated by the labour of another: the capitalist is the one who put his capital at risk. The difference is that rather than the outcomes being determined through competition in the market, the outcome of the contest is determined by a judge. The only link between the work and the remuneration comes from the prize giver, who is now in a position of judge, charitable giver, or beneficent lord and who has no obligation to any of the contestants. As a governmental policy, or approach to funding, the logic of the prize is extended into an acceptable work relation.

One might ask why inducement prizes are a problem: no one forces anyone to enter the competitions. The problem comes in with the shift in the approach to work, when prizes become a general practice. Those who don't choose to enter have fewer opportunities for contract-based work because the amount of contract-based work diminishes. The overall field changes such that people have little choice but to compete under these terms.

So in addition to the operations through which capitalists have always exploited workers – length of working day, wage theft, speed ups, charging workers for the means of production – communicative capitalism opens up new avenues for exploitation. Because the common is the general field out of which the one emerges, exploitation consists in efforts to stimulate the creative production of the field in the interest of finding, and then monetising, the one. The best example of this is the Chinese website Qidian.com, which has a million registered writers and 100 million paying members. The writers receive fractions of a cent per thousand-word update. To make enough money to survive requires writing hundreds of thousands of words a month – breaking down the division between physical and mental labour. The vast majority are stuck in the bottom. A lucky few become Platinum Writers or Big Dogs. Some of their novels have been adapted for television.

The power law distribution of nodes in complex networks (again, networks characterized by free choice growth and preferential attachment) tells us that inequality is a necessary feature of communicative capitalism. It is generated by the free flow of information through the networks and then seized and exploited in the capitalist competition for profit. If we are honest, we have to admit that there is actually no such thing as social media. Digital media is class media. Networked communication entrenches hierarchy as it uses our own choices against us.

Presenting the world fashioned by the bourgeoisie, *The Communist Manifesto* focuses on the capitalist mode of production and circulation. It highlights the connections that are established everywhere according to the compulsions of expanding markets. It brings out the constant disturbance, agitation and uncertainty as crisis becomes a mode of life. International interdependence increases under the asymmetrical conditions of colonialism. Means of production and communication are constantly improved and upgraded; new wants are created. Inequality intensifies. The bourgeoisie concentrates property in ever fewer hands and those who live by the wage find their conditions ever more precarious. Communicative capitalism is our contemporary version of this same world.

The Struggle of the Proletarianised

The Communist Manifesto gives us a vision of society split into two hostile classes of exploiters and exploited, oppressors and oppressed. All of history is a history of the struggle between them. In capitalist society the primary classes are the bourgeoisie and proletariat. 'Bourgeoisie' designates the class with resources, the owners of capital and employers of labour. 'Proletarians' are those whose survival depends on selling their labour power. Unlike peasants, they don't have their own land. Unlike small business owners, the petty bourgeoisie, they don't own their own business. Proletarians are forced to earn a wage.

Some argue today that this depiction no longer applies (if it ever did). Two sorts of reasons are typically offered. The first is that classes today are highly differentiated. Not only is there a strong middle class but there are multiple economically, socially and culturally differentiated forms of status that resist easy categorisation. The second is that identities other than those of class are more politically relevant, particularly those associated with gender, sexuality, race, ethnicity, religion and ability.

The claim regarding class differentiation misses its target. *The Communist Manifesto* does not treat the bourgeoisie and the proletariat as fixed classes. They are not demographic categories based on income. They are positions that reflect tendencies, a tendency toward capital concentration and a tendency toward dependency and immiseration. As modern industry develops, parts of the middle class sink down into the proletariat – 'the small tradespeople, shopkeepers, and retired tradesmen generally, the handicraftsmen and peasants'.[14] The ruling class itself undergoes a 'process of dissolution'. Capitalist crises, the churn and decay of industries rising and falling, threaten the existence of sectors of the bourgeoisie. So the *Manifesto* does not deny the presence of differentiated classes. It points to processes that impact everyone, benefitting the very few and proletarianising the many. In 2011, the Occupy movement produced a slogan anchored in this fact: 'We Are the Ninety-Nine Percent.'

The claim regarding the political relevance of identities other than class identities is more complex. It implies that communists assume that workers are white men, thereby erasing the histories and contributions of communists all over the world, as if there had not been communist revolutions in Asia, as if communism were not important to Third World liberation struggles, as if women were not communists. It ignores the way that some of the most visible fighters against racism have been communists and opponents of capitalism. In effect, it maps onto communist emphasis on proletarian revolution a critique more applicable to a very narrow vision of trade unionism. Nevertheless, there is something to the claim for a decline in the relevance of class politics. It marks a real historical defeat: the erosion of working-class political power and the accompanying decay of labour's political position. Defeated on the political plane – the name of this defeat is 'neoliberalism' – the Left shifted to the social and cultural terrain. It fragmented into issues and identities. On some issues and with respect to some identities, there were political advances. But by turning away from class struggle, the Left lost the capacity to defend and advance the commitments to social welfare that had resulted from this struggle in the twentieth century. Economic inequality increased. Commitment to social provisioning – education, public housing, welfare, social services – collapsed.

In the second decade of the twenty-first century, the limits of identity as an operator for politics have become clear. Identity claims no longer map clearly and cleanly onto left politics. Conservative, imperialist and capitalist positions justify themselves with recourse to identity, sometimes by emphasising national, ethnic and religious specificity and sometimes by emphasising sex, race or sexuality. Intensified focus on identity has corresponded with the reduction of the space of change to the individual such that the individual's words and attitudes appear as a primary battleground while the larger systems and structures of power recede from view. The personalisation of media under communicative capitalism amplifies these tendencies. Intense feelings circulate more easily than complex arguments (TLDR). Participating in the momentary outrage makes people feel involved even as practices of calling out and shaming undermine solidarity. A final symptom of the diminished political capacity of identity is the mutual policing of who can claim what identity under what conditions: *what gives you the right or privilege to speak as a woman, as a person of colour, as queer?* Rather than identity functioning as the ground of a claim, its evocation is contested. Identities are sites of class struggle. The concerns of working-class women are not those of female CEOs telling women to 'lean in'; the election of a woman as President or Prime Minister is not a victory for all women, as Margaret Thatcher's government made perfectly clear. In 2014 and 2015, riots in Ferguson, Missouri and Baltimore, Maryland pushed the fact of class struggle into mainstream discussions of race in the US. An African-American president did not result in material improvement in Black people's lives. Keeanga-Yamahtta Taylor writes: 'Since Obama came into office, Black median income has fallen by 10.9

percent to $33,500, compared to a 3.6 percent drop for whites, leaving their median income at $58,000.'[15]

Class politics is back. The extreme inequality communicative capitalism's complex networks generate and embed has made the struggle between oppressor and oppressed, proletariat and bourgeoisie, return to centre stage. This epic confrontation appears differently from how it did in the past. The crowds and riots marking the first decades of the twenty-first century are the new face of global class struggle. Arab Spring, Occupy movement, Chilean student protests, Montreal fees protests, Brazilian transportation and FIFA protests, Gezi Park protest, European anti-austerity protests, Black Lives Matter as well as multiple ongoing and intermittent strikes of teachers, communication workers, civil servants and medical workers all over the world are protests of the class of those proletarianised under communicative capitalism. These are not merely the defensive struggles of a middle class facing cuts to social services, wage stagnation, unemployment, foreclosure and indebtedness. They are fronts in class war under the conditions of global communicative capitalism, revolts of those whose communicative activities generate value that is expropriated from them.[16]

Demographic data supports reading the revolts of the early twenty-first century as an insurrection of the proletarianised. In an analysis of Occupy Wall Street, Ruth Milkman, Stephanie Luce and Penny Lewis find that highly educated young people were over-represented among OWS activists and supporters. Many were under-employed, indebted, or had recently lost their jobs.[17] A report based on data collected by Turkish security forces shows that over half the Gezi park protesters were in university or university graduates even as their incomes were in the bottom economic half.[18] Andre Singer, looking at the massive Brazilian protests of June 2013, likewise emphasises the predominance of young, highly educated and un- or under-employed adults.[19] In protests in the eight Brazilian state capitals, 43 per cent of protesters had college degrees. In protests in São Paolo, nearly 80 per cent had college degrees. Although these educational levels could suggest a middle-class revolt, income and occupation point in the direction of the lower and lower middle class, the bottom half of society where people are more likely to work as shop assistants, drivers, waiters, receptionists and primary school teachers than they are as technicians or administrators. To make sense of the disparity between high education and low incomes, Singer posits a new proletariat taking to the streets.

The young, educated and un- or under-employed are revolting. Communicative capitalism's intense competition decreases the return on their investment in education. As they wind up in jobs for which they are over-qualified, they push those without a college education out of the labour market entirely, thereby contributing indirectly to long-term unemployment.[20] In 2013, the occupations employing the largest numbers of people in the US were all service sector: retail sales, cashiers, food service, office workers, nursing, customer service.[21]

Alongside the large-scale movements like 2011's Occupy, the movement of the squares in Greece and Spain and the Arab Spring, there has been a wide array of strikes and actions by communicative labourers. Highly visible ones in the US include the protests of civil service workers in Wisconsin in 2011, the Chicago teachers' strike of 2012 and the Communication Workers' strike against Verizon in 2016. Globally, the strikes of the proletarianised are virtually innumerable. Here is a partial list from March 2014: public sector and airport workers in Germany; cleaners at the University of London; a telecom strike in Ghana; a sit-in at an airport in Sudan in protest over the contracting out of security jobs; teachers and education support workers in Western Australia; 7,000 doctors in South Korea opposing plans to introduce telemedicine and for-profit hospital subsidiaries; Greek civil servants, teachers, doctors and pharmacists; non-teaching staff and postal workers in India.[22] Even this partial list of ongoing, active, but still disconnected struggles supports the idea that the protests of the last few years are revolts of proletarianised communicators.

Class struggle in communicative capitalism is not expressed primarily through workplace struggles. The flexibilisation and precaritisation of work enabled by networked communication technologies spread communicative production throughout the social field. Struggles follow the workplace's own extension into every part of life via the expectation that workers are always reachable, always on. For contingent and mobile workers, phones are means of production and any place is workplace. Student, debt, housing and education protests carry on the struggle of the proletarianised as they demand socialised rather than private solutions. Those struggles that do occur at workplaces increasingly involve communicative labourers, teachers, transport workers and service sector workers.

The changes in communication and subjectivity that accompany communicative capitalism pose real problems for the organisation of the proletarianised. Inescapable demands on our attention enable images to circulate more easily than arguments, positions and demands – we can process them faster. Intense attachment to individuality, difference and uniqueness – all important in the competition for jobs and opportunities – hinder solidarity. Micro-politics, issue-politics, anarchism, one-off demos, clictivism and ironic events appear more compelling than the sustained work of party-building. Not only are they easier but they repeat communicative capitalist ideologies of individualism, publicity and participation.

Using *The Communist Manifesto* as our guide and reading these protests and revolts in terms of their setting in communicative capitalism makes them legible as the class struggle of the proletarianised. It accounts for the pervasive personal media, the people protesting, the economic position of the protesters *and* the political ambiguity of the protests. Repeating the tenets of bourgeois ideology, new proles are often individualistic. They may present themselves as post-political or anti-political (as in, for example, the Spanish movement of the squares). Some espouse libertarianism or anarchism. They have a hard time seeing themselves and uniting as a class even as their actions are the expressions of a class. But these challenges are nothing new. The *Manifesto* itself notes how competition between the workers makes it hard for them to unite and organise.

Marx does not simply link communism to the identity of the working class. He links it to working-class *movement*. In the nineteenth century, worker uprisings were pushing forward, coming together, breaking out and disrupting capital processes of value extraction. This active movement incites Marx to see in proletarian struggle more than demands for shorter working days, safer working conditions and higher wages. It is the political process of the subject of communism. The same applies today. The movement of the proletarianised all over the world is away from and against the capitalist system that fragments and exploits us, pitting us one against another for the benefit of the one percent. It is toward that emancipatory egalitarianism that goes under the name 'communism'.

The Party

Perhaps the most crucial insight of *The Communist Manifesto* is that 'class struggle is a political struggle'. Economic power expresses itself as political power, the power of a ruling class to make laws for its own benefit. Marx and Engels write: 'The executive of the modern State is but a committee for managing the common affairs of the whole bourgeoisie.' So even as *The Communist Manifesto* presents an internationalist vision of a world under capitalism, a world characterised by colonialism, dependency, resource exploitation and uneven concentrations of wealth, it argues for the conquest of political power by the proletariat, a struggle that occurs at the level of the nation-state. To win on this front, the proletariat has to organise itself as a party and acquire political supremacy.

Some readers of Marx underplay the political struggle. They emphasise strands of the *Manifesto* that suggest a kind of 'historical determinism' whereby contradictory dynamics at play in the capitalist mode of production lead inevitably to the downfall of the bourgeoisie. Capitalism's own crises disorder the whole society and endanger bourgeois property. Of course, bourgeois rule, like the capitalist system, is historical, which means that it has a beginning and will have an end. But the inevitability of the end of capitalism does not mean the automatic victory of *communism*. Communism has to be fought for, pursued, achieved. Marx links communism to the movement of the working class, giving it a specific political content. Because exploitation can only end with the abolition of wage-labour and capital, that is to say, with the abolition of property, communism must be the political goal of proletarian struggle.

The abolition of capitalism does not come about by economic destruction alone. The normal operation of the capitalist system is characterised by crises, epidemics of over-production. In the words of the *Manifesto*, 'Society suddenly finds itself put back into a state of momentary barbarism; it appears as if a famine, a universal war of devastation had cut off the supply of every means of subsistence; industry and commerce seem to be destroyed.'[23] The bourgeoisie has created a mode of production and circulation that generates crises, engenders widespread immiseration *and* calls into being the very force that will bring it down. 'Proletariat' names capitalism's self-creation of what destroys it. The proletariat is a collective subject, a force no longer dispersed in individual and local acts of smashing, sabotage and disruption, but concentrated through its struggles against the bourgeoisie.

Marx sees more than the power of the bourgeoisie and the misery of the proletariat. He recognises as well the weakness of the bourgeois and the strength of the proletariat. Capitalist society produces those who will overthrow it – the class of proletarians – and aids their development. The *Manifesto* describes how modern industry brings previously separate and isolated workers together. Improved means of communication enable workers in different industries and localities to connect with and learn from each other. As workers start to organise themselves into a class, 'and consequently into a political party', they are able to exploit divisions among the bourgeoisie and secure legislative victories (the *Manifesto* gives the example of the laws limiting the length of the working day). These victories further strengthen the working class, expanding their sense of themselves as a class.

Contemporary capitalism has refined its capacity for wealth destruction: over $34 trillion of market value was lost in the financial crisis of 2008. In the course of the recession that followed, the rich got richer and the poor poorer: the top 1 per cent captured 121 per cent of the income gains made between 2009 and 2011.[24] Not only was the 1 per cent better able to weather the crisis than the rest of us, but it was also able to increase its share. It's not just economic destruction that's at stake in the abolition of capitalism. It's bringing to an end the capitalist cycle of creative destructive – the destruction of destruction. And *this* political destruction is brought to an end by the proletariat. It is not the task of the working class organised as *workers*. They are already organised as workers in the factory, which enables them to become conscious of their material conditions and the need to combine into unions. The abolition of capitalism depends on the organisation of the proletariat as a *party*, a solidary political association that cuts across workplace, sector, region and nation. The working class *as a class* is implicated in the success or stability of capitalism. Capitalism configures the working class's struggles with the bourgeoisie. In contrast, the party takes as *its* horizon capitalism's supercession in communism. For Marx, the party is necessary because class struggle is not simply economic struggle. It's political struggle.

Yet even as Marx used the title, *The Manifesto of the Communist Party*, and even as he presents the political development of the proletariat as leading to the formation of a political party, the *Manifesto* states: 'The communists do not form a separate party opposed to the other working-class parties.'[25] This might suggest that Marx understands communists as a 'red thread' in the broader proletarian movement. A better interpretation recognises that what's at stake here is opposition. Marx is emphasising that communists work together with other working-class organisations. They share the aim of proletarian conquest of political power. The communists are the 'most advanced and resolute' of these parties, pushing the others forward and having a clear theoretical understanding of the conditions, path and ultimate results of the movement. Communists emphasise the common interests of the proletariat internationally, rather than, say, focusing on narrow concerns that a specific proletariat might share with its national bourgeoisie. To this end, communists keep before them the movement as a whole.

It is precisely because the communists are active in the broader proletarian movement that they need a clear statement of their theory: 'Abolition of private property.' When Marx was writing, not all workers' organisations prioritised the struggle for political power. Some were more interested in workers' control of factories. Not all socialists placed their hopes for radical change in the proletariat. In the middle of the nineteenth century, there were multiple socialist positions and tendencies. The last two sections of the *Manifesto* describes them, setting out the difference between these parties and the communists. While all socialists were critical of bourgeois society, some wanted to go back to a kind of agrarian feudalism. Others imagined a petty-bourgeois socialism. Marx criticises reformers, 'organisers of charity, members of societies for the prevention of cruelty to animals, temperance fanatics' and others for wanting the advantages of modern society without the costs. 'They wish for a bourgeoisie without a proletariat.'[26] He criticises as well the utopians with their 'fantastic pictures of future society'. These utopians only see the proletariat in its suffering. Because the class struggle is still in an early phase, they fail to anchor their analyses in the antagonism between bourgeoisie and proletariat and instead imagine improving society as a whole. Their goal is reconciliation. Revolution appears as a problem rather than the way forward.

While the parties and currents have changed today, the problems remain the same. The broad, churning, mediated nature of communicative capitalism brings together such an array of positions under the label of 'Left' that we oscillate between a sense that 'the Left doesn't exist' and 'the Left is whoever identifies as Left'. These are two sides of the same coin. Celebrating plurality, the former treats the fragmentation of issues and identities as a political advance, the rupturing of restrictive party politics into spaces for creativity and experimentation. Celebrating individual choice, the latter takes multiplicity to be the condition of freedom. It rejects the formulation of programmes and demands, prioritises individual experiences, values therapeutic practices of emotional reconciliation and discounts polemics, condemnation and judgement. Disconnected from class struggle, antagonism is defanged and depoliticised, reduced to interpersonal relations instead of channelled into revolutionary politics. Celebrations of plurality efface capitalism's uneven development – the fact of structural inequality – flattening out and immediatising the terrain of struggle. They obliterate differences in resources, histories and opportunities. Celebrations of individuality disavow the tensions within and between struggles, as if each individual's choice were automatically compatible with that of every other. The result is the reproduction of communicative capitalism ideologically through the reiteration of its values and politically through the failure to build a concentrated political force with the sustained capacity to confront and replace the capitalist mode of production. Instead, there are small battles, policy options and cultural interventions, victories that can be absorbed and defeats that can be forgotten.

The new cycle of struggles has demonstrated the political strength that comes from collectivity. Common names, tactics and images are bringing the fragments together, making them legible as many fronts of one struggle against capitalism. Movements against austerity, foreclosure, debt and precarity have generated new parties and strengthened left factions of older ones. Just as the *Manifesto* presents the party as an outgrowth of the movement of the workers in the battle against the bourgeoisie, so has the new sense of the importance of the party for political struggle emerged out of the struggles of the proletarianised. The party offers a political form that spans multiple levels and domains. Parties scale across local, regional, national and sometimes international levels. Rather than stuck in the local or confined by the abstractions of the global, the party is an organisational form operative on different scales; its success – electorally or otherwise – depends on this capacity. Parties carry the knowledge that comes with political experience. Whether this knowledge is local – histories of relationships, of practices, of who knows whom, what, where and how – or larger – knowledge of resource extraction and the structure of industry, of civil wars in far off places, of patterns of raced oppression, of the challenges of social reproduction, of programming, database construction and design – parties recognise the breadth and depth of knowledge important for political struggle and rule. Providing a body for a knowledge that exceeds what any one person can know, the party takes a position on that knowledge. It fits issues into a platform such that they are not so many contradictory and individual preferences but instead a broader vision for which it will fight.

The Manifesto of the Communist Party sets out such a platform. It acknowledges that the specific provisions may not be applicable everywhere. What matters is the overarching goal they are designed to achieve – the establishment of common ownership over the means of production – so as to produce a new form of association in which 'the free development of each is the condition for the free development of all'.[27]

Revolution

The Manifesto of the Communist Party is a guide for us. Its anchoring of political change in a global and historical understanding of economic production and circulation, its focus on the antagonism between proletariat and bourgeoisie at the basis of the capitalist mode of production, and its emphasis on political struggle make this nearly 200-year-old text more relevant today than it has ever been. The *Manifesto* offers a vision of an economy out of control, a class of owners concentrating wealth in its own hands, and an ever-increasing, ever-immiserated class of wage-labourers. It locates power, possibility and right in the hands of the oppressed. The oppressed are not simply exploited, deskilled and precarious. They stand up and fight back, a militant proletariat whose movement is the movement of the majority for the majority, a revolutionary class whose emancipation is the emancipation of all of society. A better world's in birth.

The strength of the proletariat comes from its economic position in production and its historical role as the agent of communism. The strength of the *Manifesto* stems from its linking of these two together such that the goal of the workers' movement is a radically changed society. Marx does not say that workers have told him this. He doesn't even present the existing socialists and communists as advocating much more than bourgeois revolution. He presents communist revolution as what the ruling class fears.

The Manifesto of the Communist Party begins and ends by describing communism as a threat: the famous opening, 'A spectre is haunting Europe – the spectre of communism', and the saucy close: 'Let the ruling classes tremble at a communistic revolution.' The ruling class is not as strong as they want us to think. They are afraid of us, the workers, the many, the oppressed. The power of the idea of communism derives from the effect it has on the proletariat's class enemies, an effect that precedes the existence of the proletariat organised as a party of communists. Marx seizes and occupies that fear. He doesn't say, 'oh, let's not call ourselves communists because that is too controversial'. He doubles down, championing the term *and* declaring the need for the forcible overthrow of all existing conditions. This boldness is yet another reason the *Manifesto* is an indispensable guide for us today.

Today the ruling class's fear of communism returns in surprising places. For example, in a speech at the Democratic National Convention where Hillary Clinton became the party's nominee for President of the United States, Barack Obama positioned fascists, communists, jihadists, and homegrown demagogues as threats to American values. Communists – nearly 30 years after the collapse of the Soviet Union and capitalist democracy's declaration of victory – are as dangerous as terrorists. Why did Obama feel the need to call out communists as a threat? Because 'communist', as Marx well knew, is the name that we have for a society without exploitation, a society where people collectively determine how to produce for their common needs – as well as the name for someone who fights to realise such a society. At a time of ever-increasing economic inequality and state violence as well as of rising popular militancy and increased support for socialism, Obama was trying to exorcise a spectre that continues to haunt the ruling class. The fact of this continued haunting is our signal to champion the name 'communist' again.

Across the globe, the movements of the proletarianised have opened up the perspective of revolution. People are rioting, demonstrating and organising against capitalist dispossession of their labour, lives and futures. Because capitalism's system of dispossession operates through the wage, debt, privatisation, enclosure, theft, colonisation, financialisation and racialised state violence, the movements of the proletarianised mobilise a broad, international, array of people and concerns.

Describing the unfitness of bourgeoisie to be the ruling class, Marx emphasises the sinking conditions of the working class. The producer can no longer produce but must be fed. In the words of the *Manifesto*, 'Society can no longer live under this bourgeoisie, in other words, its existence is no longer compatible with society.'[28] The winner-take-all character of the twenty-first century economy brings this point home. Communicative capitalism produces many losers, few winners. Ever more corporations replace workers with technology. Taking place on social media and through digital networks, our social relations themselves become the private property of another.

The incompatibility of capitalism with society is most undeniable when we look at anthropogenic climate change. What the *Manifesto* calls 'Modern Industry' has set off atmospheric warming that is leading to temperatures not seen on the planet for millions of years. This warming has a series of interconnected effects. Melting glaciers, thawing permafrost, sea-level rise, desertification, weather instability and species loss are some of them. The repercussions for human society include the loss of hundreds of thousands of miles of coastline, including coastal cities and communities; the loss of arable and pasture land; the loss of fresh water; the loss of ways of life; increasing numbers of refugees as people move to higher, cooler and more fertile areas; and increasing conflict as resource wars escalate. Global capital has proven unfit for addressing climate change. Investment in extractive industries and fossil fuels continues. Coal mining, oil drilling and fracking continue. Large-scale commodity production and shipping continue. That one city, state or country might bring carbon emissions under control – while certainly a step in the right direction – is irrelevant from the standpoint of overall warming. Perhaps its carbon-emitting industries were shipped elsewhere. Perhaps another country expanded its own drilling operations. Climate change forces us to acknowledge that not all communities, economies or ways of life are compatible. A capitalist economy premised on production for the sake of private capital accumulation stands in fundamental conflict with the planning and transformation necessary for dismantling the industries and practices that contribute to planetary warming. Forcing that change is the political challenge of our time – which is why a popular slogan is 'System change, not climate change'.

Some readers of Marx view him as advocating a kind of 'productivism' where the point of proletarian revolution is eliminating the constraints ('fetters') on production caused by bourgeois relations of production. The idea here is that bourgeois society cannot absorb all that it produces. The miserable wages of the workers, 'vicissistudes of competition', overproduction and 'fluctuations of the market' create a contradictory situation where an economic arrangement of production devolves into and becomes indistinguishable from a mode of economic destruction. When production is in the hands of the proletariat, the destruction and waste occasioned by competition will come to an end. Production will then be able to develop more rapidly. The *Manifesto* points in this direction when it says that the proletariat will use its political supremacy 'to increase the total productive forces as rapidly as possible'.[29]

A better reading of Marx recognises that while continued industrial development may have made sense in the nineteenth century, what industrial development means has changed. In the twenty-first century, it directs us toward the global fact of uneven development and the impact of this unevenness on production, trade, modes of life and capacity to adapt to and mitigate the effects of a changing climate. The relations of production and circulation in bourgeois society today are fetters; they prevent the development of modes of production and circulation liberated from fossil fuels. They foreclose possibilities for large-scale planning. The contemporary capitalist economy privileges expensive and fanciful high-tech solutions that let the very rich continue to increase their wealth while the rest of us are relegated to sacrifice zones.

As if to lessen the blow of letting the market determine which communities live and which ones die, the Obama administration – again relying on the contests characteristic of communicative capitalism – created the National Disaster Resilience Competition. Communities were invited to compete for funds that would enable them to recover from and plan for disasters. Some win; some lose. Not only is the competition separated from the industries and practices that contribute to global warming, but treating aid as if it were a prize means that losers are owed nothing, entitled to nothing, deserving of nothing but their own demise.

The Marxist theorist John Bellamy Foster writes:

> In the Marxian view updated for our time, capitalism has not only inverted the world, it threatens to drive a stake through its heart. The world is not moving under capitalism toward the *unity* of humanity and nature but toward a dangerous *separation*: one, though, that represents, in the alienated context of class society, an 'unconscious socialist tendency,' in that it gives rise to the necessity of revolutionary human intervention.[30]

Today the movement of the proletarianised is the movement of all whom capitalism deprives of a future, all whose work and lives are expropriated from them by a 1 per cent that presumes that the rest of us are either for them or non-existent. Those proletarianised by climate change are thus those whose land is becoming uninhabitable and whose lives are becoming unliveable. All over the world – on Pacific islands that will be submerged by century's end, in African and Middle Eastern countries scorched by rising temperatures, in territories inhabited by native, indigenous, and First Nations people witnessing the unfolding calamity of species loss, and in global cities where millions encounter undrinkable water and unbreathable air – the proletarianised appear with new faces, new demands, and new certainty that the only way forward is together, collectively. The struggle around climate change is the struggle for communism.

To sum up, the *Communist Manifesto* is a practical guide for us, a hundred years after the Russian Revolution, because the interests of the capitalist class remain opposed to those of the rest of us, the proletarianised. Society is fundamentally divided. They are our enemy. Their flourishing depends on our misery. The only way this will change in a way that will benefit us is if we force it. The fact of the fundamental division between the capitalist class and the rest of us makes revolutionary force necessary – and it makes it right.

Notes

1. See Hal Draper, *The Adventures of the Communist Manifesto*, Alameda, CA: Center for Socialist History, 2004.
2. See p. 102.
3. Nadezhda Krupskaya, 'How Lenin Studied Marx' (1933). www.marxists.org/archive/krupskaya/works/howleninstudiedmarx.htm.
4. Karl Kautsy, 'To What Extent is the *Communist Manifesto* Obsolete?' (1905) www.marxists.org/archive/kautsky/1904/xx/manifesto.htm.
5. See p. 51.
6. See the afterword to *The Communist Manifesto: A Road Map to History's Most Important Political Document*, Karl Marx and Friedrich Engels, edited by Phil Gasper, Chicago, IL: Haymarket Books, 2005.
7. 'Richest 62 people as wealthy as half the world's population, says Oxfam', *Guardian*, 18 January 2016.
8. See p. 76.
9. Enda Brophy and Grieg de Peuter, 'Labors of Mobility: Communicative Capitalism and the Smartphone Cybertariat', *Theories of the Mobile Internet*, eds Andrew Herman, Jan Hadlaw and Thom Swiss, New York, Routledge, 2015.
10. Jaron Lanier, *Who Owns the Future*, New York, Simon and Schuster, 2013, p. 15.
11. Fred Turner, 'On Accelerationism,' *Public Books*, 1 September 2016. http://www.publicbooks.org/nonfiction/on-accelerationism
12. Peter Haynes and M-H. Carolyn Nguyen, 'Rebalancing Socio-Economic Asymmetry in a Data-Driven Economy', *The Global Information Technology Report 2014*, Geneva, Switzerland: World Economic Forum, 2014, 70, weforum.org.
13. 'Strategy for American Innovation', whitehouse.gov.
14. See p. 61.
15. Keeanga-Yamahtta Taylor, *From #BlackLivesMatter to Black Liberation*, Chicago, IL: Haymarket Books, 2016, p. 11.
16. Nick Dyer-Witherford, *Cyber-Proletariat: Global Labour in the Digital Vortex*, London: Pluto Press, 2015. See also Christian Fuch's 'Labor in informational capitalism and on the internet,' *The Information Society* 26, 2010: 179–96.

17. Ruth Milkman, Stephanie Luce and Penny Lewis, 'Changing the Subject: A Bottom-Up Account of Occupy Wall Street in New York City', p. 4. (The Murphy Institute CUNY, 2013), available at http://sps.cuny.edu/filestore/1/5/7/1_a05051d2117901d/1571_92f562221b8041e.pdf.
18. '78 percent of Gezi Park protest detainees were Alevis: Report', *Hurriyet Daily News* 25 November 2013, available at www.hurriyetdailynews.com/78-percent-of-gezi-park-protest-detainees-were-alevis-report-.aspx?pageID=238&nID=58496&NewsCatID=341.
19. Andre Singer, 'Rebellion in Brazil', *New Left* Review, 85, Jan–Feb 2014.
20. Jordan Weissmann, '53% of Recent College Grads are Jobless or Underemployed – How?', *The Atlantic* 23 April 2012, available at www.theatlantic.com/business/archive/2012/04/53-of-recent-college-grads-are-jobless-or-underemployed-how/256237/; and 'College Grads Taking Low-Wage Jobs Displace Less Educated', *Bloomberg* 23 March 2014, available at www.bloomberg.com/news/2014-03-06/college-grads-taking-low-wage-jobs-displace-less-educated.html.
21. 'Occupational Employment and Wages – May 2013' (Bureau of Labour Statistics, US Department of Labor, 2014), available at www.bls.gov/news.release/pdf/ocwage.pdf.
22. See the overview provided by the World Socialist Web Site here: www.wsws.org/en/articles/2014/03/28/wkrs-m28.html.
23. See p. 58.
24. Bonnie Kavoussi, 'Top One Percent Captured 121 Percent of All Income Gains During Recovery's First Years: Study', *Huffington Post*, 2 February 2013.
25. See p. 70.
26. See p. 94.
27. See p. 84.
28. See p. 68.
29. See p. 82.
30. John Bellamy Foster, 'Marxism in the Anthropocene: Dialectical Rifts on the Left', *International Critical Thought* 2016, vol. 6, no. 3 (393–421) p. 407.

2
MANIFESTO OF THE COMMUNIST PARTY

A spectre is haunting Europe – the spectre of communism. All the powers of old Europe have entered into a holy alliance to exorcise this spectre: Pope and Tsar, Metternich and Guizot, French Radicals and German police-spies.

Where is the party in opposition that has not been decried as communistic by its opponents in power? Where is the opposition that has not hurled back the branding reproach of communism, against the more advanced opposition parties, as well as against its reactionary adversaries?

Two things result from this fact:

1. Communism is already acknowledged by all European powers to be itself a power.
2. It is high time that communists should openly, in the face of the whole world, publish their views, their aims, their tendencies, and meet this nursery tale of the spectre of communism with a manifesto of the party itself.

To this end, communists of various nationalities have assembled in London and sketched the following manifesto, to be published in the English, French, German, Italian, Flemish and Danish languages.

I Bourgeois and Proletarians[1]

The history of all hitherto existing society[2] is the history of class struggles.

Freeman and slave, patrician and plebeian, lord and serf, guild-master[3] and journeyman, in a word, oppressor and oppressed, stood in constant opposition to one another, carried on an uninterrupted, now hidden, now open fight, a fight that each time ended,

1. By bourgeoisie is meant the class of modern capitalists, owners of the means of social production and employers of wage labour. By proletariat, the class of modern wage-labourers who, having no means of production of their own, are reduced to selling their labour power in order to live. [Engels, 1888 English edition]
2. That is, all *written* history. In 1847, the pre-history of society, the social organisation existing previous to recorded history, all but unknown. Since then, August von Haxthausen (1792–1866) discovered common ownership of land in Russia, Georg Ludwig von Maurer proved it to be the social foundation from which all Teutonic races started in history, and, by and by, village communities were found to be, or to have been, the primitive form of society everywhere from India to Ireland. The inner organisation of this primitive communistic society was laid bare, in its typical form, by Lewis Henry Morgan's (1818–1861) crowning discovery of the true nature of the gens and its relation to the tribe. With the dissolution of the primeval communities, society begins to be differentiated into separate and finally antagonistic classes. I have attempted to retrace this dissolution in *The Origin of the Family, Private Property, and the State*, second edition, Stuttgart, 1886. [Engels, 1888 English edition and 1890 German edition (with the last sentence omitted)]
3. Guild-master, that is, a full member of a guild, a master within, not a head of a guild. [Engels, 1888 English edition]

either in a revolutionary reconstitution of society at large, or in the common ruin of the contending classes.

In the earlier epochs of history, we find almost everywhere a complicated arrangement of society into various orders, a manifold gradation of social rank. In ancient Rome we have patricians, knights, plebeians, slaves; in the Middle Ages, feudal lords, vassals, guild-masters, journeymen, apprentices, serfs; in almost all of these classes, again, subordinate gradations.

The modern bourgeois society that has sprouted from the ruins of feudal society has not done away with class antagonisms. It has but established new classes, new conditions of oppression, new forms of struggle in place of the old ones.

Our epoch, the epoch of the bourgeoisie, possesses, however, this distinct feature: it has simplified class antagonisms. Society as a whole is more and more splitting up into two great hostile camps, into two great classes directly facing each other – bourgeoisie and proletariat.

From the serfs of the Middle Ages sprang the chartered burghers of the earliest towns. From these burgesses the first elements of the bourgeoisie were developed.

The discovery of America, the rounding of the Cape, opened up fresh ground for the rising bourgeoisie. The East-Indian and Chinese markets, the colonisation of America, trade with the colonies, the increase in the means of exchange and in commodities generally, gave to commerce, to navigation, to industry, an impulse never before known, and thereby, to the revolutionary element in the tottering feudal society, a rapid development.

The feudal system of industry, in which industrial production was monopolised by closed guilds, now no longer sufficed for the growing wants of the new markets. The manufacturing system took its place. The guild-masters were pushed on one side by the manufacturing middle class; division of labour between the different corporate guilds vanished in the face of division of labour in each single workshop.

Meantime the markets kept ever growing, the demand ever rising. Even manufacture no longer sufficed. Thereupon, steam and machinery revolutionised industrial production. The place of manufacture was taken by the giant, modern industry; the place of the industrial middle class by industrial millionaires, the leaders of the whole industrial armies, the modern bourgeois.

Modern industry has established the world market, for which the discovery of America paved the way. This market has given an immense development to commerce, to navigation, to communication by land. This development has, in its turn, reacted on the extension of industry; and in proportion as industry, commerce, navigation, railways extended, in the same proportion the bourgeoisie developed, increased its capital, and pushed into the background every class handed down from the Middle Ages.

We see, therefore, how the modern bourgeoisie is itself the product of a long course of development, of a series of revolutions in the modes of production and of exchange.

Each step in the development of the bourgeoisie was accompanied by a corresponding political advance of that class. An oppressed class under the sway of the feudal nobility, an armed and self-governing association in the medieval commune[4]: here independent urban republic (as in Italy and Germany); there taxable 'third estate' of the monarchy (as in France); afterwards, in the period of manufacturing proper, serving either the semi-feudal or the absolute monarchy as a counterpoise against the nobility, and, in fact, cornerstone of the great monarchies in general, the bourgeoisie has at last, since the establishment of modern industry and of the world market, conquered for itself, in the modern representative state, exclusive political sway. The executive of the modern state is but

4. This was the name given their urban communities by the townsmen of Italy and France, after they had purchased or conquered their initial rights of self-government from their feudal lords. [Engels, 1890 German edition]

'Commune' was the name taken in France by the nascent towns even before they had conquered from their feudal lords and masters local self-government and political rights as the 'Third Estate'. Generally speaking, for the economical development of the bourgeoisie, England is here taken as the typical country, for its political development, France. [Engels, 1888 English edition]

a committee for managing the common affairs of the whole bourgeoisie.

The bourgeoisie, historically, has played a most revolutionary part.

The bourgeoisie, wherever it has got the upper hand, has put an end to all feudal, patriarchal, idyllic relations. It has pitilessly torn asunder the motley feudal ties that bound man to his 'natural superiors', and has left remaining no other nexus between man and man than naked self-interest, than callous 'cash payment'. It has drowned the most heavenly ecstasies of religious fervour, of chivalrous enthusiasm, of philistine sentimentalism, in the icy water of egotistical calculation. It has resolved personal worth into exchange value, and in place of the numberless indefeasible chartered freedoms, has set up that single, unconscionable freedom – Free Trade. In one word, for exploitation, veiled by religious and political illusions, it has substituted naked, shameless, direct, brutal exploitation.

The bourgeoisie has stripped of its halo every occupation hitherto honoured and looked up to with reverent awe. It has converted the physician, the lawyer, the priest, the poet, the man of science, into its paid wage-labourers.

The bourgeoisie has torn away from the family its sentimental veil, and has reduced the family relation to a mere money relation.

The bourgeoisie has disclosed how it came to pass that the brutal display of vigour in the Middle Ages, which reactionaries so much admire, found its fitting complement in the most slothful indolence. It has been the first to show what man's activity can bring about. It has accomplished wonders far surpassing Egyptian pyramids, Roman aqueducts, and Gothic cathedrals; it has conducted expeditions that put in the shade all former exoduses of nations and crusades.

The bourgeoisie cannot exist without constantly revolutionising the instruments of production, and thereby the relations of production, and with them the whole relations of society. Conservation of the old modes of production in unaltered form, was, on the contrary, the first condition of existence for all earlier industrial classes. Constant revolutionising of production, uninterrupted disturbance of all social conditions, everlasting uncertainty and agitation distinguish the bourgeois epoch from all earlier ones. All fixed, fast-frozen relations, with their train of ancient and venerable prejudices and opinions, are swept away, all new-formed ones become antiquated before they can ossify. All that is solid melts into air, all that is holy is profaned, and man is at last compelled to face with sober senses, his real conditions of life, and his relations with his kind.

The need of a constantly expanding market for its products chases the bourgeoisie over the entire surface of the globe. It must nestle everywhere, settle everywhere, establish connections everywhere.

The bourgeoisie has through its exploitation of the world market given a cosmopolitan character to production and consumption in every country. To the great chagrin of reactionists, it has drawn from under the feet of industry the national ground on which it stood. All old-established national industries have been destroyed or are daily being destroyed. They are dislodged by new industries, whose introduction becomes a life and death question for all civilised nations, by industries that no longer work up indigenous raw material, but raw material drawn from the remotest zones; industries whose products are consumed, not only at home, but in every quarter of the globe. In place of the old wants, satisfied by the production of the country, we find new wants, requiring for their satisfaction the products of distant lands and climes. In place of the old local and national seclusion and self-sufficiency, we have intercourse in every direction, universal inter-dependence of nations. And as in material, so also in intellectual production. The intellectual creations of individual nations become common property. National one-sidedness and narrow-mindedness become more and more impossible, and from the numerous national and local literatures, there arises a world literature.

The bourgeoisie, by the rapid improvement of all instruments of production, by the immensely facilitated means of communication, draws all, even the most barbarian, nations into civilisation. The cheap prices of commodities are the heavy artillery with which it batters down all Chinese walls, with which it forces the barbarians' intensely obstinate hatred of foreigners to capitulate. It compels all nations, on pain of extinction, to adopt the bourgeois mode of production; it compels them to introduce what it calls civilisation into their midst, i.e., to become bourgeois themselves. In one word, it creates a world after its own image.

The bourgeoisie has subjected the country to the rule of the towns. It has created enormous cities, has greatly increased the urban population as compared with the rural, and has thus rescued a considerable part of the population from the idiocy of rural life. Just as it has made the country dependent on the towns, so it has made barbarian and semi-barbarian countries dependent on the civilised ones, nations of peasants on nations of bourgeois, the East on the West.

The bourgeoisie keeps more and more doing away with the scattered state of the population, of the means of production, and of property. It has agglomerated population, centralised the means of production, and has concentrated property in a few hands. The necessary consequence of this was political centralisation. Independent, or but loosely connected provinces, with separate interests, laws, governments, and systems of taxation, became lumped together into one nation, with one government, one code of laws, one national class-interest, one frontier, and one customs-tariff.

The bourgeoisie, during its rule of scarce 100 years, has created more massive and more colossal productive forces than have all preceding generations together. Subjection of nature's forces to man, machinery, application of chemistry to industry and agriculture, steam-navigation, railways, electric telegraphs, clearing of whole continents for cultivation, canalisation of rivers, whole populations conjured out of the ground – what earlier century had even a presentiment that such productive forces slumbered in the lap of social labour?

We see then: the means of production and of exchange, on whose foundation the bourgeoisie built itself up, were generated in feudal society. At a certain stage in the development of these means of production and of exchange, the conditions under which feudal society produced and exchanged, the feudal organisation of agriculture and manufacturing industry, in one word, the feudal relations of property became no longer compatible with the already developed productive forces; they became so many fetters. They had to be burst asunder; they were burst asunder.

Into their place stepped free competition, accompanied by a social and political constitution adapted in it, and the economic and political sway of the bourgeois class.

A similar movement is going on before our own eyes. Modern bourgeois society, with its relations of production, of exchange and of property, a society that has conjured up such gigantic means of production and of exchange, is like the sorcerer who is no longer able to control the powers of the nether world whom he has called up by his spells. For many a decade past the history of industry and commerce is but the history of the revolt of modern productive forces against modern conditions of production, against the property relations that are the conditions for the existence of the bourgeois and of its rule. It is enough to mention the commercial crises that by their periodical return put the existence of the entire bourgeois society on its trial, each time more threateningly. In these crises, a great part not only of the existing products, but also of the previously created productive forces, are periodically destroyed. In these crises, there breaks out an epidemic that, in all earlier epochs, would have seemed an absurdity – the epidemic of over-production. Society suddenly finds itself put back into a state of momentary barbarism; it appears as if a famine, a universal war of devastation, had cut off the supply of every means of subsistence; industry and commerce seem to be destroyed; and why? Because there is too much civilisation, too much means of subsistence, too much industry, too much commerce. The productive forces at the disposal of society no longer tend to further the development of the conditions of bourgeois property; on the contrary, they have become too powerful for these conditions, by which they are fettered, and so soon as they overcome these fetters, they bring disorder into the whole of bourgeois society, endanger the existence of bourgeois property. The conditions of bourgeois society are too narrow to comprise the wealth created by them. And how does the bourgeoisie get over these crises? On the one hand by enforced destruction of a mass of productive forces; on the other, by the conquest of new markets, and by the more thorough exploitation of the old ones. That is to say, by paving the way for more extensive and more destructive crises, and by diminishing the means whereby crises are prevented.

The weapons with which the bourgeoisie felled feudalism to the ground are now turned against the bourgeoisie itself.

But not only has the bourgeoisie forged the weapons that bring death to itself; it has also called into existence the men who are to wield those weapons – the modern working class – the proletarians.

In proportion as the bourgeoisie, i.e., capital, is developed, in the same proportion is the proletariat, the modern working class, developed – a class of labourers, who live only so long as they find work, and who find work only so long as their labour increases capital. These labourers, who must sell themselves piecemeal, are a commodity, like every other article of commerce, and are consequently exposed to all the vicissitudes of competition, to all the fluctuations of the market.

Owing to the extensive use of machinery, and to the division of labour, the work of the proletarians has lost all individual character, and, consequently, all charm for the workman. He becomes an appendage of the machine, and it is only the most simple, most monotonous, and most easily acquired knack, that is required of him. Hence, the cost of production of a workman is restricted, almost entirely, to the means of subsistence that he requires for maintenance, and for the propagation of his race. But the price of a commodity, and therefore also of labour, is equal to its cost of production. In proportion, therefore, as the repulsiveness of the work increases, the wage decreases. Nay more, in proportion as the use of machinery and division of labour increases, in the same proportion the burden of toil also increases, whether by prolongation of the working hours, by the increase of the work exacted in a given time or by increased speed of machinery, etc.

Modern industry has converted the little workshop of the patriarchal master into the great factory of the industrial capitalist. Masses of labourers, crowded into the factory, are organised like soldiers. As privates of the industrial army they are placed under the command of a perfect hierarchy of officers and sergeants. Not only are they slaves of the bourgeois class, and of the bourgeois state; they are daily and hourly enslaved by the machine, by the overlooker, and, above all, by the individual bourgeois manufacturer himself. The more openly this despotism proclaims gain to be its end and aim, the more petty, the more hateful and the more embittering it is.

The less the skill and exertion of strength implied in manual labour, in other words, the more modern industry becomes developed, the more is the labour of men superseded by that of women. Differences of age and sex have no longer any distinctive social validity for the working class. All are instruments of labour, more or less expensive to use, according to their age and sex.

No sooner is the exploitation of the labourer by the manufacturer, so far, at an end, that he receives his wages in cash, than he is set upon by the other portions of the bourgeoisie, the landlord, the shopkeeper, the pawnbroker, etc.

The lower strata of the middle class – the small tradespeople, shopkeepers, and retired tradesmen generally, the handicraftsmen and peasants – all these sink gradually into the proletariat, partly because their diminutive capital does not suffice for the scale on which modern industry is carried on, and is swamped in the competition with the large capitalists, partly because their specialised skill is rendered worthless by new methods of production. Thus the proletariat is recruited from all classes of the population.

The proletariat goes through various stages of development. With its birth begins its struggle with the bourgeoisie. At first the contest is carried on by individual labourers, then by the workpeople of a factory, then by the operative of one trade, in one locality, against the individual bourgeois who directly exploits them. They direct their attacks not against the bourgeois conditions of production, but against the instruments of production themselves; they destroy imported wares that compete with their labour, they smash to pieces machinery, they set factories ablaze, they seek to restore by force the vanished status of the workman of the Middle Ages.

At this stage, the labourers still form an incoherent mass scattered over the whole country, and broken up by their mutual competition. If anywhere they unite to form more compact bodies, this is not yet the consequence of their own active union, but of the union of the bourgeoisie, which class, in order to attain its own political ends, is compelled to set the whole proletariat in motion, and is moreover yet, for a time, able to do so. At this stage, therefore, the proletarians do not fight their enemies, but the enemies of their enemies, the remnants of absolute monarchy, the landowners, the non-industrial bourgeois, the petty bourgeois. Thus, the whole historical movement is concentrated in the hands of the bourgeoisie; every victory so obtained is a victory for the bourgeoisie.

But with the development of industry, the proletariat not only increases in number; it becomes concentrated in greater masses, its strength grows, and it feels that strength more. The various interests and conditions of life within the ranks of the proletariat are more and more equalised, in proportion as machinery obliterates all distinctions of labour, and nearly everywhere reduces wages to the same low level. The growing competition among the bourgeois, and the resulting commercial crises, make the wages of the workers ever more fluctuating. The increasing improvement of machinery, ever more rapidly developing, makes their livelihood more and more precarious; the collisions between individual workmen and individual bourgeois take more and more the character of collisions between two classes. Thereupon, the workers begin to form combinations (trades unions) against the bourgeois; they club together in order to keep up the rate of wages; they found permanent associations in order to make provision beforehand for these occasional revolts. Here and there, the contest breaks out into riots.

Now and then the workers are victorious, but only for a time. The real fruit of their battles lies, not in the immediate result, but in the ever expanding union of the workers. This union is helped on by the improved means of communication that are created by modern industry, and that place the workers of different localities in contact with one another. It was just this contact that was needed to centralise the numerous local struggles, all of the same character, into one national struggle between classes. But every class struggle is a political struggle. And that union, to attain which the burghers of the Middle Ages, with their miserable highways, required centuries, the modern proletarian, thanks to railways, achieve in a few years.

This organisation of the proletarians into a class, and, consequently into a political party, is continually being upset again by the competition between the workers themselves. But it ever rises up again, stronger, firmer, mightier. It compels legislative recognition of particular interests of the workers, by taking advantage of the divisions among the bourgeoisie itself. Thus, the ten-hours' bill in England was carried.

Altogether collisions between the classes of the old society further, in many ways, the course of development of the proletariat. The bourgeoisie finds itself involved in a constant battle. At first with the aristocracy; later on, with those portions of the bourgeoisie itself, whose interests have become antagonistic to the progress of industry; at all time with the bourgeoisie of foreign countries. In all these battles, it sees itself compelled to appeal to the proletariat, to ask for help, and thus, to drag it into the political arena. The bourgeoisie itself, therefore, supplies the proletariat with its own elements of political and general education, in other words, it furnishes the proletariat with weapons for fighting the bourgeoisie.

Further, as we have already seen, entire sections of the ruling class are, by the advance of industry, precipitated into the proletariat, or are at least threatened in their conditions of existence. These also supply the proletariat with fresh elements of enlightenment and progress.

Finally, in times when the class struggle nears the decisive hour, the progress of dissolution going on within the ruling class, in fact within the whole range of old society, assumes such a violent, glaring character, that a small section of the ruling class cuts itself adrift, and joins the revolutionary class, the class that holds the future in its hands. Just as, therefore, at an earlier period, a section of the nobility went over to the bourgeoisie, so now a portion of the bourgeoisie goes over to the proletariat, and in particular, a portion of the bourgeois ideologists, who have raised themselves to the level of comprehending theoretically the historical movement as a whole.

Of all the classes that stand face to face with the bourgeoisie today, the proletariat alone is a really revolutionary class. The other classes decay and finally disappear in the face of modern industry; the proletariat is its special and essential product.

The lower middle class, the small manufacturer, the shopkeeper, the artisan, the peasant, all these fight against the bourgeoisie, to save from extinction their existence as fractions of the middle class. They are therefore not revolutionary, but conservative. Nay more, they are reactionary, for they try to roll back the wheel of history. If by chance, they are revolutionary, they are only so in view of their impending transfer into the proletariat; they thus defend not their present, but their future interests, they desert their own standpoint to place themselves at that of the proletariat.

The 'dangerous class', [*lumpenproletariat*] the social scum, that passively rotting mass thrown off by the lowest layers of the old society, may, here and there, be swept into the movement by a proletarian revolution; its conditions of life, however, prepare it far more for the part of a bribed tool of reactionary intrigue.

In the condition of the proletariat, those of old society at large are already virtually swamped. The proletarian is without property; his relation to his wife and children has no longer anything in common with the bourgeois family relations; modern industry labour, modern subjection to capital, the same in England as in France, in America as in Germany, has stripped him of every trace of national character. Law, morality, religion, are to him so many bourgeois prejudices, behind which lurk in ambush just as many bourgeois interests.

All the preceding classes that got the upper hand sought to fortify their already acquired status by subjecting society at large to their conditions of appropriation. The proletarians cannot become masters of the productive forces of society, except by abolishing their own previous mode of appropriation, and thereby also every other previous mode of appropriation. They have nothing of their own to secure and to fortify; their mission is to destroy all previous securities for, and insurances of, individual property.

All previous historical movements were movements of minorities, or in the interest of minorities. The proletarian movement is the self-conscious, independent movement of the immense majority, in the interest of the immense majority. The proletariat, the lowest stratum of our present society, cannot stir, cannot raise itself up, without the whole superincumbent strata of official society being sprung into the air.

Though not in substance, yet in form, the struggle of the proletariat with the bourgeoisie is at first a national struggle. The proletariat of each country must, of course, first of all settle matters with its own bourgeoisie.

In depicting the most general phases of the development of the proletariat, we traced the more or less veiled civil war, raging within existing society, up to the point where that war breaks out into open revolution, and where the violent overthrow of the bourgeoisie lays the foundation for the sway of the proletariat.

Hitherto, every form of society has been based, as we have already seen, on the antagonism of oppressing and oppressed classes. But in order to oppress a class, certain conditions must be assured to it under which it can, at least, continue its slavish existence. The serf, in the period of serfdom, raised himself to membership in the commune, just as the petty bourgeois, under the yoke of the feudal absolutism, managed to develop into a bourgeois. The modern labourer, on the contrary, instead of rising with the process of industry, sinks deeper and deeper below the conditions of existence of his own class. He becomes a pauper, and pauperism develops more rapidly than population and wealth. And here it becomes evident, that the bourgeoisie is unfit any longer to be the ruling class in society, and to impose its conditions of existence upon society as an over-riding law. It is unfit to rule because it is incompetent to assure an existence to its slave within his slavery, because it cannot help letting him sink into such a state, that it has to feed him, instead of being fed by him. Society can no longer live under this bourgeoisie, in other words, its existence is no longer compatible with society.

The essential conditions for the existence and for the sway of the bourgeois class is the formation and augmentation of capital; the condition for capital is wage labour. Wage labour rests exclusively on competition between the labourers. The advance of industry, whose involuntary promoter is the bourgeoisie, replaces the isolation of the labourers, due to competition, by the revolutionary combination, due to association. The development of modern industry, therefore, cuts from under its feet the very foundation on which the bourgeoisie produces and appropriates products. What the bourgeoisie therefore produces, above all, are its own grave-diggers. Its fall and the victory of the proletariat are equally inevitable.

II Proletarians and Communists

In what relation do the communists stand to the proletarians as a whole? The communists do not form a separate party opposed to the other working-class parties.

They have no interests separate and apart from those of the proletariat as a whole.

They do not set up any sectarian principles of their own, by which to shape and mould the proletarian movement.

The communists are distinguished from the other working-class parties by this only:

1. In the national struggles of the proletarians of the different countries, they point out and bring to the front the common interests of the entire proletariat, independently of all nationality.
2. In the various stages of development which the struggle of the working class against the bourgeoisie has to pass through, they always and everywhere represent the interests of the movement as a whole.

The communists, therefore, are on the one hand, practically, the most advanced and resolute section of the working-class parties of every country, that section which pushes forward all others; on the other hand, theoretically, they have over the great mass of the proletariat the advantage of clearly understanding the lines of march, the conditions, and the ultimate general results of the proletarian movement.

The immediate aim of the communists is the same as that of all other proletarian parties: formation of the proletariat into a class, overthrow of the bourgeois supremacy, conquest of political power by the proletariat.

The theoretical conclusions of the communists are in no way based on ideas or principles that have been invented, or discovered, by this or that would-be universal reformer.

They merely express, in general terms, actual relations springing from an existing class struggle, from a historical movement going on under our very eyes. The abolition of existing property relations is not at all a distinctive feature of communism.

All property relations in the past have continually been subject to historical change consequent upon the change in historical conditions.

The French Revolution, for example, abolished feudal property in favour of bourgeois property.

The distinguishing feature of communism is not the abolition of property generally, but the abolition of bourgeois property. But modern bourgeois private property is the final and most complete expression of the system of producing and appropriating products, that is based on class antagonisms, on the exploitation of the many by the few.

In this sense, the theory of the communists may be summed up in the single sentence: Abolition of private property.

We communists have been reproached with the desire of abolishing the right of personally acquiring property as the fruit of a man's own labour, which property is alleged to be the groundwork of all personal freedom, activity and independence.

Hard-won, self-acquired, self-earned property! Do you mean the property of petty artisan and of the small peasant, a form of property that preceded the bourgeois form? There is no need to abolish that; the development of industry has to a great extent already destroyed it, and is still destroying it daily.

Or do you mean the modern bourgeois private property?

But does wage labour create any property for the labourer? Not a bit. It creates capital, i.e., that kind of property which exploits wage labour, and which cannot increase except upon condition of begetting a new supply of wage labour for fresh exploitation. Property, in its present form, is based on the antagonism of capital and wage labour. Let us examine both sides of this antagonism.

To be a capitalist, is to have not only a purely personal, but a social *status* in production. Capital is a collective product, and only by the united action of many members, nay, in the last resort, only by the united action of all members of society, can it be set in motion.

Capital is therefore not only personal; it is a social power.

When, therefore, capital is converted into common property, into the property of all members of society, personal property is not thereby transformed into social property. It is only the social character of the property that is changed. It loses its class character.

Let us now take wage labour.

The average price of wage labour is the minimum wage, i.e., that quantum of the means of subsistence which is absolutely requisite to keep the labourer in bare existence as a labourer. What, therefore, the wage-labourer appropriates by means of his labour, merely suffices to prolong and reproduce a bare existence. We by no means intend to abolish this personal appropriation of the products of labour, an appropriation that is made for the maintenance and reproduction of human life, and that leaves no surplus wherewith to command the labour of others. All that we want to do away with is the miserable character of this appropriation, under which the labourer lives merely to increase capital, and is allowed to live only in so far as the interest of the ruling class requires it.

In bourgeois society, living labour is but a means to increase accumulated labour. In communist society, accumulated labour is but a means to widen, to enrich, to promote the existence of the labourer.

In bourgeois society, therefore, the past dominates the present; in communist society, the present dominates the past. In bourgeois society capital is independent and has individuality, while the living person is dependent and has no individuality.

And the abolition of this state of things is called by the bourgeois, abolition of individuality and freedom! And rightly so. The abolition of bourgeois individuality, bourgeois independence, and bourgeois freedom is undoubtedly aimed at.

By freedom is meant, under the present bourgeois conditions of production, free trade, free selling and buying.

But if selling and buying disappears, free selling and buying disappears also. This talk about free selling and buying, and all the other 'brave words' of our bourgeois about freedom in general, have a meaning, if any, only in contrast with restricted selling and buying, with the fettered traders of the Middle Ages, but have no meaning when opposed to the communistic abolition of buying and selling, of the bourgeois conditions of production, and of the bourgeoisie itself.

You are horrified at our intending to do away with private property. But in your existing society, private property is already done away with for nine-tenths of the population; its existence for the few is solely due to its non-existence in the hands of those nine-tenths. You reproach us, therefore, with intending to do away with a form of property, the necessary condition for whose existence is the non-existence of any property for the immense majority of society.

In one word, you reproach us with intending to do away with your property. Precisely so; that is just what we intend.

From the moment when labour can no longer be converted into capital, money, or rent, into a social power capable of being monopolised, i.e., from the moment when individual property can no longer be transformed into bourgeois property, into capital, from that moment, you say, individuality vanishes.

You must, therefore, confess that by 'individual' you mean no other person than the bourgeois, than the middle-class owner of property. This person must, indeed, be swept out of the way, and made impossible.

Communism deprives no man of the power to appropriate the products of society; all that it does is to deprive him of the power to subjugate the labour of others by means of such appropriations.

It has been objected that upon the abolition of private property, all work will cease, and universal laziness will overtake us.

According to this, bourgeois society ought long ago to have gone to the dogs through sheer idleness; for those of its members who work, acquire nothing, and those who acquire anything do not work. The whole of this objection is but another expression of the tautology: that there can no longer be any wage labour when there is no longer any capital.

All objections urged against the communistic mode of producing and appropriating material products, have, in the same way, been urged against the communistic mode of producing and appropriating intellectual products. Just as, to the bourgeois, the disappearance of class property is the disappearance of production itself, so the disappearance of class culture is to him identical with the disappearance of all culture.

That culture, the loss of which he laments, is, for the enormous majority, a mere training to act as a machine.

But don't wrangle with us so long as you apply, to our intended abolition of bourgeois property, the standard of your bourgeois notions of freedom, culture, law, etc. Your very ideas are but the outgrowth of the conditions of your bourgeois production and bourgeois property, just as your jurisprudence is but the will of your class made into a law for all, a will whose essential character and direction are determined by the economical conditions of existence of your class.

The selfish misconception that induces you to transform into eternal laws of nature and of reason, the social forms springing from your present mode of production and form of property – historical relations that rise and disappear in the progress of production – this misconception you share with every ruling class that has preceded you. What you see clearly in the case of ancient property, what you admit in the case of feudal property, you are of course forbidden to admit in the case of your own bourgeois form of property.

Abolition [*Aufhebung*] of the family! Even the most radical flare up at this infamous proposal of the communists.

On what foundation is the present family, the bourgeois family, based? On capital, on private gain. In its completely developed form, this family exists only among the bourgeoisie. But this state of things finds its complement in the practical absence of the family among the proletarians, and in public prostitution.

The bourgeois family will vanish as a matter of course when its complement vanishes, and both will vanish with the vanishing of capital.

Do you charge us with wanting to stop the exploitation of children by their parents? To this crime we plead guilty.

But, you say, we destroy the most hallowed of relations, when we replace home education by social.

And your education! Is not that also social, and determined by the social conditions under which you educate, by the intervention direct or indirect, of society, by means of schools, etc.? The communists have not invented the intervention of society in education; they do but seek to alter the character of that intervention, and to rescue education from the influence of the ruling class.

The bourgeois clap-trap about the family and education, about the hallowed co-relation of parents and child, becomes all the more disgusting, the more, by the action of modern industry, all the family ties among the proletarians are torn asunder, and their children transformed into simple articles of commerce and instruments of labour.

But you communists would introduce community of women, screams the bourgeoisie in chorus.

The bourgeois sees in his wife a mere instrument of production. He hears that the instruments of production are to be exploited in common, and, naturally, can come to no other conclusion than that the lot of being common to all will likewise fall to the women.

He has not even a suspicion that the real point aimed at is to do away with the status of women as mere instruments of production.

For the rest, nothing is more ridiculous than the virtuous indignation of our bourgeois at the community of women which, they pretend, is to be openly and officially established by the communists. The communists have no need to introduce community of women; it has existed almost from time immemorial.

Our bourgeois, not content with having wives and daughters of their proletarians at their disposal, not to speak of common prostitutes, take the greatest pleasure in seducing each other's wives.

Bourgeois marriage is, in reality, a system of wives in common and thus, at the most, what the communists might possibly be reproached with is that they desire to introduce, in substitution for a hypocritically concealed, an openly legalised community of women. For the rest, it is self-evident that the abolition of the present system of production must bring with it the abolition of the community of women springing from that system, i.e., of prostitution both public and private.

The communists are further reproached with desiring to abolish countries and nationality.

The working men have no country. We cannot take from them what they have not got. Since the proletariat must first of all acquire political supremacy, must rise to be the leading class of the nation, must constitute itself *the* nation, it is so far, itself national, though not in the bourgeois sense of the word.

National differences and antagonism between peoples are daily more and more vanishing, owing to the development of the bourgeoisie, to freedom of commerce, to the world market, to uniformity in the mode of production and in the conditions of life corresponding thereto.

The supremacy of the proletariat will cause them to vanish still faster. United action, of the leading civilised countries at least, is one of the first conditions for the emancipation of the proletariat.

In proportion as the exploitation of one individual by another will also be put an end to, the exploitation of one nation by another will also be put an end to. In proportion as the antagonism between classes within the nation vanishes, the hostility of one nation to another will come to an end.

The charges against communism made from a religious, a philosophical and, generally, from an ideological standpoint, are not deserving of serious examination.

Does it require deep intuition to comprehend that man's ideas, views, and conception, in one word, man's consciousness, changes with every change in the conditions of his material existence, in his social relations and in his social life?

What else does the history of ideas prove, than that intellectual production changes its character in proportion as material production is changed? The ruling ideas of each age have ever been the ideas of its ruling class.

When people speak of the ideas that revolutionise society, they do but express the fact that within the old society the elements of a new one have been created, and that the dissolution of the old ideas keeps even pace with the dissolution of the old conditions of existence.

When the ancient world was in its last throes, the ancient religions were overcome by Christianity. When Christian ideas succumbed in the eighteenth century to rationalist ideas, feudal society fought its death battle with the then revolutionary bourgeoisie. The ideas of religious liberty and freedom of conscience merely gave expression to the sway of free competition within the domain of knowledge.

'Undoubtedly,' it will be said, 'religious, moral, philosophical, and juridical ideas have been modified in the course of historical development. But religion, morality, philosophy, political science, and law, constantly survived this change.'

'There are, besides, eternal truths, such as Freedom, Justice, etc., that are common to all states of society. But communism abolishes eternal truths, it abolishes all religion, and all morality, instead of constituting them on a new basis; it therefore acts in contradiction to all past historical experience.'

What does this accusation reduce itself to? The history of all past society has consisted in the development of class antagonisms, antagonisms that assumed different forms at different epochs.

But whatever form they may have taken, one fact is common to all past ages, viz., the exploitation of one part of society by the other. No wonder, then, that the social consciousness of past ages, despite all the multiplicity and variety it displays, moves within certain common forms, or general ideas, which cannot completely vanish except with the total disappearance of class antagonisms.

The communist revolution is the most radical rupture with traditional relations; no wonder that its development involved the most radical rupture with traditional ideas.

But let us have done with the bourgeois objections to communism.

We have seen above, that the first step in the revolution by the working class is to raise the proletariat to the position of ruling class to win the battle of democracy.

The proletariat will use its political supremacy to wrest, by degree, all capital from the bourgeoisie, to centralise all instruments of production in the hands of the state, i.e., of the proletariat organised as the ruling class; and to increase the total productive forces as rapidly as possible.

Of course, in the beginning, this cannot be effected except by means of despotic inroads on the rights of property, and on the conditions of bourgeois production; by means of measures, therefore, which appear economically insufficient and untenable, but which, in the course of the movement, outstrip themselves, necessitate further inroads upon the old social order, and are unavoidable as a means of entirely revolutionising the mode of production.

These measures will, of course, be different in different countries.

Nevertheless, in most advanced countries, the following will be pretty generally applicable:

1. Abolition of property in land and application of all rents of land to public purposes.
2. A heavy progressive or graduated income tax.

3. Abolition of all rights of inheritance.
4. Confiscation of the property of all emigrants and rebels.
5. Centralisation of credit in the banks of the state, by means of a national bank with state capital and an exclusive monopoly.
6. Centralisation of the means of communication and transport in the hands of the state.
7. Extension of factories and instruments of production owned by the state; the bringing into cultivation of waste-lands, and the improvement of the soil generally in accordance with a common plan.
8. Equal liability of all to work. Establishment of industrial armies, especially for agriculture.
9. Combination of agriculture with manufacturing industries; gradual abolition of all the distinction between town and country by a more equable distribution of the populace over the country.
10. Free education for all children in public schools. Abolition of children's factory labour in its present form. Combination of education with industrial production, etc, etc.

When, in the course of development, class distinctions have disappeared, and all production has been concentrated in the hands of a vast association of the whole nation, the public power will lose its political character. Political power, properly so called, is merely the organised power of one class for oppressing another. If the proletariat during its contest with the bourgeoisie is compelled, by the force of circumstances, to organise itself as a class, if, by means of a revolution, it makes itself the ruling class, and, as such, sweeps away by force the old conditions of production, then it will, along with these conditions, have swept away the conditions for the existence of class antagonisms and of classes generally, and will thereby have abolished its own supremacy as a class.

In place of the old bourgeois society, with its classes and class antagonisms, we shall have an association, in which the free development of each is the condition for the free development of all.

III Socialist and Communist Literature

1. Reactionary Socialism

A. Feudal Socialism

Owing to their historical position, it became the vocation of the aristocracies of France and England to write pamphlets against modern bourgeois society. In the French Revolution of July 1830, and in the English reform agitation, these aristocracies again succumbed to the hateful upstart. Thenceforth, a serious political struggle was altogether out of the question. A literary battle alone remained possible. But even in the domain of literature the old cries of the restoration period had become impossible.[5]

In order to arouse sympathy, the aristocracy was obliged to lose sight, apparently, of its own interests, and to formulate their indictment against the bourgeoisie in the interest of the exploited working class alone. Thus, the aristocracy took their revenge by singing lampoons on their new masters and whispering in his ears sinister prophesies of coming catastrophe.

In this way arose feudal socialism: half lamentation, half lampoon; half an echo of the past, half menace of the future; at times, by its bitter, witty and incisive criticism, striking the bourgeoisie to the very heart's

5. Not the English Restoration (1660–89), but the French Restoration (1814–30). [Engels, 1888 German edition]

core; but always ludicrous in its effect, through total incapacity to comprehend the march of modern history.

The aristocracy, in order to rally the people to them, waved the proletarian alms-bag in front for a banner. But the people, so often as it joined them, saw on their hindquarters the old feudal coats of arms, and deserted with loud and irreverent laughter.

One section of the French Legitimists and 'Young England' exhibited this spectacle.

In pointing out that their mode of exploitation was different to that of the bourgeoisie, the feudalists forget that they exploited under circumstances and conditions that were quite different and that are now antiquated. In showing that, under their rule, the modern proletariat never existed, they forget that the modern bourgeoisie is the necessary offspring of their own form of society.

For the rest, so little do they conceal the reactionary character of their criticism that their chief accusation against the bourgeois amounts to this, that under the bourgeois *régime* a class is being developed which is destined to cut up root and branch the old order of society.

What they upbraid the bourgeoisie with is not so much that it creates a proletariat as that it creates a *revolutionary* proletariat.

In political practice, therefore, they join in all coercive measures against the working class; and in ordinary life, despite their high-falutin phrases, they stoop to pick up the golden apples dropped from the tree of industry, and to barter truth, love, and honour, for traffic in wool, beetroot-sugar, and potato spirits.[6]

As the parson has ever gone hand in hand with the landlord, so has clerical socialism with feudal socialism.

Nothing is easier than to give Christian asceticism a socialist tinge. Has not Christianity declaimed against private property, against marriage, against the state? Has it not preached in the place of these, charity and poverty, celibacy and mortification of the flesh, monastic life and Mother Church? Christian socialism is but the holy water with which the priest consecrates the heart-burnings of the aristocrat.

B. Petty-Bourgeois Socialism

The feudal aristocracy was not the only class that was ruined by the bourgeoisie, not the only class whose conditions of existence pined and perished in the atmosphere of modern bourgeois society. The medieval burgesses and the small peasant proprietors were

6. This applies chiefly to Germany, where the landed aristocracy and squirearchy have large portions of their estates cultivated for their own account by stewards, and are, moreover, extensive beetroot-sugar manufacturers and distillers of potato spirits. The wealthier British aristocracy are, as yet, rather above that; but they, too, know how to make up for declining rents by lending their names to floaters or more or less shady joint-stock companies. [Engels, 1888 German edition]

the precursors of the modern bourgeoisie. In those countries which are but little developed, industrially and commercially, these two classes still vegetate side by side with the rising bourgeoisie.

In countries where modern civilisation has become fully developed, a new class of petty bourgeois has been formed, fluctuating between proletariat and bourgeoisie, and ever renewing itself as a supplementary part of bourgeois society. The individual members of this class, however, are being constantly hurled down into the proletariat by the action of competition, and, as modern industry develops, they even see the moment approaching when they will completely disappear as an independent section of modern society, to be replaced in manufactures, agriculture and commerce, by overlookers, bailiffs and shopmen.

In countries like France, where the peasants constitute far more than half of the population, it was natural that writers who sided with the proletariat against the bourgeoisie should use, in their criticism of the bourgeois *régime*, the standard of the peasant and petty bourgeois, and from the standpoint of these intermediate classes, should take up the cudgels for the working class. Thus arose petty-bourgeois socialism. Sismondi was the head of this school, not only in France but also in England.

This school of socialism dissected with great acuteness the contradictions in the conditions of modern production. It laid bare the hypocritical apologies of economists. It proved, incontrovertibly, the disastrous effects of machinery and division of labour; the concentration of capital and land in a few hands; overproduction and crises; it pointed out the inevitable ruin of the petty bourgeois and peasant, the misery of the proletariat, the anarchy in production, the crying inequalities in the distribution of wealth, the industrial war of extermination between nations, the dissolution of old moral bonds, of the old family relations, of the old nationalities.

In its positive aims, however, this form of socialism aspires either to restoring the old means of production and of exchange, and with them the old property relations, and the old society, or to cramping the modern means of production and of exchange within the framework of the old property relations that have been, and were bound to be, exploded by those means. In either case, it is both reactionary and utopian.

Its last words are: corporate guilds for manufacture; patriarchal relations in agriculture.

Ultimately, when stubborn historical facts had dispersed all intoxicating effects of self-deception, this form of socialism ended in a miserable hangover.

C. German or 'True' Socialism

The socialist and communist literature of France, a literature that originated under the pressure of a bourgeoisie in power, and that was the expression of the struggle against this power, was introduced into Germany at a time when the bourgeoisie, in that country, had just begun its contest with feudal absolutism.

German philosophers, would-be philosophers, and *beaux esprits* (men of letters), eagerly seized on this literature, only forgetting, that when these writings immigrated from France into Germany, French social conditions had not immigrated along with them. In contact with German social conditions, this French literature lost all its immediate practical significance and assumed a purely literary aspect. Thus, to the German philosophers of the eighteenth century, the demands of the first French Revolution were nothing more than the demands of 'Practical Reason' in general, and the utterance of the will of the revolutionary French bourgeoisie signified, in their eyes, the laws of pure Will, of Will as it was bound to be, of true human Will generally.

The work of the German *literati* consisted solely in bringing the new French ideas into harmony with their ancient philosophical conscience, or rather, in annexing the French ideas without deserting their own philosophic point of view.

This annexation took place in the same way in which a foreign language is appropriated, namely, by translation.

It is well known how the monks wrote silly lives of Catholic saints *over* the manuscripts on which the classical works of ancient heathendom had been written. The German *literati* reversed this process with the profane French literature. They wrote their philosophical nonsense beneath the French original. For instance, beneath the French criticism of the economic functions of money, they wrote 'Alienation of Humanity', and beneath the French criticism of the bourgeois state they wrote 'Dethronement of the Category of the General', and so forth.

The introduction of these philosophical phrases at the back of the French historical criticisms, they dubbed 'Philosophy of Action', 'True Socialism', 'German Science of Socialism', 'Philosophical Foundation of Socialism', and so on.

The French socialist and communist literature was thus completely emasculated. And, since it ceased in the hands of the German to express the struggle of one class with the other, he felt conscious of having overcome 'French one-sidedness' and of representing, not true requirements, but the requirements of Truth; not the interests of the proletariat, but the interests of Human Nature, of Man in general, who belongs to no class, has no reality, who exists only in the misty realm of philosophical fantasy.

This German socialism, which took its schoolboy task so seriously and solemnly, and extolled its poor stock-in-trade in such a mountebank fashion, meanwhile gradually lost its pedantic innocence.

The fight of the Germans, and especially of the Prussian bourgeoisie, against feudal aristocracy and absolute monarchy, in other words, the liberal movement, became more earnest.

By this, the long wished-for opportunity was offered to 'True' Socialism of confronting the political movement with the socialist demands, of hurling the traditional anathemas against liberalism, against representative government, against bourgeois competition, bourgeois freedom of the press, bourgeois legislation, bourgeois liberty and equality, and of preaching to the masses that they had nothing to gain, and everything to lose, by this bourgeois movement. German socialism forgot, in the nick of time, that the French criticism, whose silly echo it was, presupposed the existence of modern bourgeois society, with its corresponding economic conditions of existence, and the political constitution adapted thereto, the very things whose attainment was the object of the pending struggle in Germany.

To the absolute governments, with their following of parsons, professors, country squires, and officials, it served as a welcome scarecrow against the threatening bourgeoisie.

It was a sweet finish, after the bitter pills of flogging and bullets, with which these same governments, just at that time, dosed the German working-class risings.

While this 'True' Socialism thus served the government as a weapon for fighting the German bourgeoisie, it, at the same time, directly represented a reactionary interest, the interest of German philistines.

In Germany, the *petty-bourgeois* class, a relic of the sixteenth century, and since then constantly cropping up again under the various forms, is the real social basis of the existing state of things.

To preserve this class is to preserve the existing state of things in Germany. The industrial and political supremacy of the bourgeoisie threatens it with certain destruction – on the one hand, from the concentration of capital; on the other, from the rise of a revolutionary proletariat. 'True' Socialism appeared to kill these two birds with one stone. It spread like an epidemic.

The robe of speculative cobwebs, embroidered with flowers of rhetoric, steeped in the dew of sickly sentiment, this transcendental robe in which the German socialists wrapped their sorry 'eternal truths', all skin and bone, served to wonderfully increase the sale of their goods amongst such a public.

And on its part German socialism recognised, more and more, its own calling as the bombastic representative of the petty-bourgeois philistine.

It proclaimed the German nation to be the model nation, and the German petty philistine to be the typical man. To every villainous meanness of this model man, it gave a hidden, higher, socialistic interpretation, the exact contrary of its real character. It went to the extreme length of directly opposing the 'brutally destructive' tendency of communism, and of proclaiming its supreme and impartial contempt of all class struggles. With very few exceptions, all the so-called socialist and communist publications that now (1847) circulate in Germany belong to the domain of this foul and enervating literature.[7]

2. Conservative or Bourgeois Socialism

A part of the bourgeoisie is desirous of redressing social grievances in order to secure the continued existence of bourgeois society.

To this section belong economists, philanthropists, humanitarians, improvers of the condition of the working class, organisers of charity, members of societies for the prevention of cruelty to animals, temperance fanatics, hole-and-corner reformers of every imaginable kind. This form of socialism has, moreover, been worked out into complete systems.

We may cite Proudhon's *Philosophie de la Misère* as an example of this form.

The socialistic bourgeois want all the advantages of modern social conditions without the struggles and dangers necessarily resulting therefrom. They desire the existing state of society, minus its revolutionary and disintegrating elements. They wish for a bourgeoisie without a proletariat. The bourgeoisie naturally conceives the world in which it is supreme to be the best; and bourgeois socialism develops this

7. The revolutionary storm of 1848 swept away this whole shabby tendency and cured its protagonists of the desire to dabble in socialism. The chief representative and classical type of this tendency is Mr Karl Gruen. [Engels, 1888 German edition]

comfortable conception into various more or less complete systems. In requiring the proletariat to carry out such a system, and thereby to march straightaway into the social New Jerusalem, it but requires in reality, that the proletariat should remain within the bounds of existing society, but should cast away all its hateful ideas concerning the bourgeoisie.

A second, and more practical, but less systematic, form of this socialism sought to depreciate every revolutionary movement in the eyes of the working class by showing that no mere political reform, but only a change in the material conditions of existence, in economical relations, could be of any advantage to them. By changes in the material conditions of existence, this form of socialism, however, by no means understands abolition of the bourgeois relations of production, an abolition that can be effected only by a revolution, but administrative reforms, based on the continued existence of these relations; reforms, therefore, that in no respect affect the relations between capital and labour, but, at the best, lessen the cost, and simplify the administrative work, of bourgeois government.

Bourgeois socialism attains adequate expression when, and only when, it becomes a mere figure of speech.

Free trade: for the benefit of the working class. Protective duties: for the benefit of the working class. Prison reform: for the benefit of the working class.

This is the last word and the only seriously meant word of bourgeois socialism.

It is summed up in the phrase: the bourgeois is a bourgeois – for the benefit of the working class.

3. Critical-Utopian Socialism and Communism

We do not here refer to that literature which, in every great modern revolution, has always given voice to the demands of the proletariat, such as the writings of Babeuf and others.

The first direct attempts of the proletariat to attain its own ends, made in times of universal excitement, when feudal society was being overthrown, necessarily failed, owing to the then undeveloped state of the proletariat, as well as to the absence of the economic conditions for its emancipation, conditions that had yet to be produced, and could be produced by the impending bourgeois epoch alone. The revolutionary literature that accompanied these first movements of the proletariat had necessarily a reactionary character. It inculcated universal asceticism and social levelling in its crudest form.

The socialist and communist systems, properly so called, those of Saint-Simon, Fourier, Owen, and others, spring into existence in the early undeveloped period, described above, of the struggle between proletariat and bourgeoisie (see Section I: Bourgeois and Proletarians).

The founders of these systems see, indeed, the class antagonisms, as well as the action of the decomposing elements in the prevailing form of society. But the proletariat, as yet in its infancy, offers to them the spectacle of a class without any historical initiative or any independent political movement.

Since the development of class antagonism keeps even pace with the development of industry, the economic situation, as they find it, does not as yet offer to them the material conditions for the emancipation of the proletariat. They therefore search after a new social science, after new social laws, that are to create these conditions.

Historical action is to yield to their personal inventive action; historically created conditions of emancipation to fantastic ones; and the gradual, spontaneous class organisation of the proletariat to an organisation of society especially contrived by these inventors. Future history resolves itself, in their eyes, into the propaganda and the practical carrying out of their social plans.

In the formation of their plans, they are conscious of caring chiefly for the interests of the working class, as being the most suffering class. Only from the point of view of being the most suffering class does the proletariat exist for them.

The undeveloped state of the class struggle, as well as their own surroundings, causes socialists of this kind to consider themselves far superior to all class antagonisms. They want to improve the condition of every member of society, even that of the most favoured. Hence, they habitually appeal to society at large, without the distinction of class; nay, by preference, to the ruling class. For how can people, when once they understand their system, fail to see in it the best possible plan of the best possible state of society?

Hence, they reject all political, and especially all revolutionary action; they wish to attain their ends by peaceful means, necessarily doomed to failure, and by the force of example, to pave the way for the new social Gospel.

Such fantastic pictures of future society, painted at a time when the proletariat is still in a very undeveloped state and has but a fantastic conception of its own position, correspond with the first instinctive yearnings of that class for a general reconstruction of society.

But these socialist and communist publications contain also a critical element. They attack every principle of existing society. Hence, they are full of the most valuable materials for the enlightenment of the working class. The practical measures proposed in them – such as the abolition of the distinction between town and country, of the family, of the carrying on of industries for the account of private individuals, and of the wage system, the proclamation of social harmony, the conversion of the function of the state into a mere superintendence of production – all these proposals point solely to the disappearance of class antagonisms which were, at that time, only just cropping up, and which, in these publications, are recognised in their earliest indistinct and undefined forms only. These proposals, therefore, are of a purely utopian character.

The significance of critical-utopian socialism and communism bears an inverse relation to historical development. In proportion as the modern class struggle develops and takes definite shape, this fantastic standing apart from the contest, these fantastic attacks on it, lose all practical value and all theoretical justification. Therefore, although the originators of these systems were, in many respects, revolutionary, their disciples have, in every case, formed mere reactionary sects. They hold fast by the original views of their masters, in opposition to the progressive historical development of the proletariat. They, therefore, endeavour, and that consistently, to deaden the class struggle and to reconcile the class antagonisms. They still dream of experimental realisation of their social utopias, of founding isolated 'phalanstères', of establishing 'Home Colonies', or setting up a 'Little Icaria'[8] – duodecimo editions of the New Jerusalem

8. *Phalanstères* were socialist colonies on the plan of Charles Fourier; *Icaria* was the name given by Cabet to his utopia and, later on, to his American communist colony. [Engels, 1888 English edition]

'Home Colonies' were what Owen called his communist model societies. *Phalanstères* was the name of the public palaces planned by Fourier. *Icaria* was the name given to the utopian land of fancy, whose communist institutions Cabet portrayed. [Engels, 1890 German edition]

– and to realise all these castles in the air, they are compelled to appeal to the feelings and purses of the bourgeois. By degrees, they sink into the category of the reactionary [or] conservative socialists depicted above, differing from these only by more systematic pedantry, and by their fanatical and superstitious belief in the miraculous effects of their social science.

They, therefore, violently oppose all political action on the part of the working class; such action, according to them, can only result from blind unbelief in the new Gospel.

The Owenites in England, and the Fourierists in France, respectively, oppose the Chartists and the *Réformistes*.

IV Position of the Communists in Relation to the Various Existing Opposition Parties

Section II has made clear the relations of the communists to the existing working-class parties, such as the Chartists in England and the Agrarian Reformers in America.

The communists fight for the attainment of the immediate aims, for the enforcement of the momentary interests of the working class; but in the movement of the present, they also represent and take care of the future of that movement. In France, the communists ally with the Social-Democrats[9] against the conservative and radical bourgeoisie, reserving, however, the right to take up a critical position in regard to phrases and illusions traditionally handed down from the great Revolution.

In Switzerland, they support the Radicals, without losing sight of the fact that this party consists of antagonistic elements, partly of Democratic Socialists, in the French sense, partly of radical bourgeois.

In Poland, they support the party that insists on an agrarian revolution as the prime condition for

9. The party then represented in parliament by Ledru-Rollin, in literature by Louis Blanc, in the daily press by the *Réforme*. The name of Social-Democracy signifies, with these its inventors, a section of the Democratic or Republican Party more or less tinged with socialism. [Engels, English edition 1888]

national emancipation, that party which fomented the insurrection of Cracow in 1846.

In Germany, they fight with the bourgeoisie whenever it acts in a revolutionary way, against the absolute monarchy, the feudal squirearchy, and the petty bourgeoisie.

But they never cease, for a single instant, to instil into the working class the clearest possible recognition of the hostile antagonism between bourgeoisie and proletariat, in order that the German workers may straightaway use, as so many weapons against the bourgeoisie, the social and political conditions that the bourgeoisie must necessarily introduce along with its supremacy, and in order that, after the fall of the reactionary classes in Germany, the fight against the bourgeoisie itself may immediately begin.

The communists turn their attention chiefly to Germany, because that country is on the eve of a bourgeois revolution that is bound to be carried out under more advanced conditions of European civilisation and with a much more developed proletariat than that of England was in the seventeenth, and France in the eighteenth century, and because the bourgeois revolution in Germany will be but the prelude to an immediately following proletarian revolution.

In short, the communists everywhere support every revolutionary movement against the existing social and political order of things.

In all these movements, they bring to the front, as the leading question in each, the property question, no matter what its degree of development at the time.

Finally, they labour everywhere for the union and agreement of the democratic parties of all countries.

The communists disdain to conceal their views and aims. They openly declare that their ends can be attained only by the forcible overthrow of all existing social conditions. Let the ruling classes tremble at a communistic revolution. The proletarians have nothing to lose but their chains. They have a world to win.

WORKING MEN OF ALL COUNTRIES, UNITE!

3
APPENDIX: PREFACES TO VARIOUS LANGUAGE EDITIONS

The 1872 German Edition

The Communist League, an international association of workers, which could of course be only a secret one, under conditions obtaining at the time, commissioned us, the undersigned, at the Congress held in London in November 1847, to write for publication a detailed theoretical and practical programme for the party. Such was the origin of the following manifesto, the manuscript of which travelled to London to be printed a few weeks before the February Revolution. First published in German, it has been republished in that language in at least twelve different editions in Germany, England, and America. It was published in English for the first time in 1850 in the *Red Republican*, London, translated by Miss Helen Macfarlane, and in 1871 in at least three different translations in America. The French version first appeared in Paris shortly before the June insurrection of 1848, and recently in

Le Socialiste of New York. A new translation is in the course of preparation. A Polish version appeared in London shortly after it was first published in Germany. A Russian translation was published in Geneva in the sixties. Into Danish, too, it was translated shortly after its appearance.

However much that state of things may have altered during the last 25 years, the general principles laid down in the *Manifesto* are, on the whole, as correct today as ever. Here and there, some detail might be improved. The practical application of the principles will depend, as the *Manifesto* itself states, everywhere and at all times, on the historical conditions for the time being existing, and, for that reason, no special stress is laid on the revolutionary measures proposed at the end of Section II. That passage would, in many respects, be very differently worded today. In view of the gigantic strides of modern industry since 1848, and of the accompanying improved and extended organisation of the working class, in view of the practical experience gained, first in the February Revolution, and then, still more, in the Paris Commune, where the proletariat for the first time held political power for two whole months, this programme has in some details been antiquated. One thing especially was proved by the Commune, viz., that 'the working class cannot simply lay hold of ready-made state machinery, and wield it for its own purposes'. (See *The Civil War in France: Address of the General Council of the International*

Working Men's Association, 1871, where this point is further developed.) Further, it is self-evident that the criticism of socialist literature is deficient in relation to the present time, because it comes down only to 1847; also that the remarks on the relation of the communists to the various opposition parties (Section IV), although, in principle still correct, yet in practice are antiquated, because the political situation has been entirely changed, and the progress of history has swept from off the Earth the greater portion of the political parties there enumerated.

But then, the *Manifesto* has become a historical document which we have no longer any right to alter. A subsequent edition may perhaps appear with an introduction bridging the gap from 1847 to the present day; but this reprint was too unexpected to leave us time for that.

Karl Marx and Friedrich Engels
24 June 1872, London

The 1882 Russian Edition

The first Russian edition of the *Manifesto of the Communist Party*, translated by Bakunin, was published early in the sixties by the printing office of the Kolokol. Then the West could see in it (the Russian edition of the *Manifesto*) only a literary curiosity. Such a view would be impossible today.

What a limited field the proletarian movement occupied at that time (December 1847) is most clearly shown by the last section: the position of the communists in relation to the various opposition parties in various countries. Precisely Russia and the United States are missing here. It was the time when Russia constituted the last great reserve of all European reaction, when the United States absorbed the surplus proletarian forces of Europe through immigration. Both countries provided Europe with raw materials and were at the same time markets for the sale of its industrial products. Both were, therefore, in one way of another, pillars of the existing European system.

How very different today. Precisely European immigration fitted North American for a gigantic agricultural production, whose competition is shaking the very foundations of European landed property – large and small. At the same time, it enabled the United States to exploit its tremendous industrial resources with an energy and on a scale that must shortly break the industrial monopoly of Western Europe, and especially of England, existing up to now. Both circumstances react in a revolutionary manner upon America itself. Step by step, the small and middle land ownership of the farmers, the basis of the whole political constitution, is succumbing to the competition of giant farms; at the same time, a mass industrial proletariat and a fabulous concentration of capital funds are developing for the first time in the industrial regions.

And now Russia! During the Revolution of 1848–49, not only the European princes, but the European bourgeois as well, found their only salvation from the proletariat just beginning to awaken in Russian intervention. The Tsar was proclaimed the chief of European reaction. Today, he is a prisoner of war of the revolution in Gatchina, and Russia forms the vanguard of revolutionary action in Europe.

The *Communist Manifesto* had, as its object, the proclamation of the inevitable impending dissolution of modern bourgeois property. But in Russia we find, face-to-face with the rapidly flowering capitalist swindle and bourgeois property, just beginning to develop, more than half the land owned in common by the peasants. Now the question is: can the Russian *obshchina*, though greatly undermined, yet a form of primeval common ownership of land, pass directly to the higher form of communist common ownership? Or, on the contrary, must it first pass through the same process of dissolution such as constitutes the historical evolution of the West?

The only answer to that possible today is this: If the Russian Revolution becomes the signal for a proletarian revolution in the West, so that both complement each other, the present Russian common ownership of land may serve as the starting point for a communist development.

Karl Marx and Friedrich Engels
21 January 1882, London

The 1883 German Edition

The preface to the present edition I must, alas, sign alone. Marx, the man to whom the whole working class of Europe and America owes more than to any one else – rests at Highgate Cemetery and over his grave the first grass is already growing. Since his death [13 March 1883], there can be even less thought of revising or supplementing the *Manifesto*. But I consider it all the more necessary again to state the following expressly:

The basic thought running through the *Manifesto* – that economic production, and the structure of society of every historical epoch necessarily arising therefrom, constitute the foundation for the political and intellectual history of that epoch; that consequently (ever since the dissolution of the primaeval communal ownership of land) all history has been a history of class struggles, of struggles between exploited and exploiting, between dominated and dominating classes at various stages of social evolution; that this struggle, however, has now reached a stage where the exploited and oppressed class (the proletariat) can no longer emancipate itself from the class which exploits and oppresses it (the bourgeoisie), without at the same time forever freeing the whole of society from exploitation, oppression, class struggles – this basic thought belongs solely and exclusively to Marx.*

* 'This proposition,' I wrote in the preface to the English translation, 'which, in my opinion, is destined to do for history what Darwin's theory has done for biology, we both of us, had been

I have already stated this many times; but precisely now is it necessary that it also stand in front of the *Manifesto* itself.

Friedrich Engels
28 June 1883, London

The 1888 English Edition

The *Manifesto* was published as the platform of the Communist League, a working men's association, first exclusively German, later on international, and under the political conditions of the Continent before 1848, unavoidably a secret society. At a Congress of the League, held in November 1847, Marx and Engels were commissioned to prepare a complete theoretical and practical party programme. Drawn up in German, in January 1848, the manuscript was sent to the printer in London a few weeks before the French Revolution of 24 February. A French translation was brought out in Paris shortly before the insurrection of June 1848. The first English translation, by Miss Helen Macfarlane, appeared in George Julian Harney's *Red*

---

gradually approaching for some years before 1845. How far I had independently progressed towards it is best shown by my *Conditions of the Working Class in England*. But when I again met Marx at Brussels, in spring 1845, he had it already worked out and put it before me in terms almost as clear as those in which I have stated it here.'

Republican, London, 1850. A Danish and a Polish edition had also been published.

The defeat of the Parisian insurrection of June 1848 – the first great battle between proletariat and bourgeoisie – drove again into the background, for a time, the social and political aspirations of the European working class. Thenceforth, the struggle for supremacy was, again, as it had been before the Revolution of February, solely between different sections of the propertied class; the working class was reduced to a fight for political elbow-room, and to the position of extreme wing of the middle-class Radicals. Wherever independent proletarian movements continued to show signs of life, they were ruthlessly hunted down. Thus the Prussian police hunted out the Central Board of the Communist League, then located in Cologne. The members were arrested and, after 18 months' imprisonment, they were tried in October 1852. This celebrated 'Cologne Communist Trial' lasted from 4 October till 12 November; seven of the prisoners were sentenced to terms of imprisonment in a fortress, varying from three to six years. Immediately after the sentence, the League was formally dissolved by the remaining members. As to the *Manifesto*, it seemed henceforth doomed to oblivion.

When the European workers had recovered sufficient strength for another attack on the ruling classes, the International Working Men's Association sprang up. But this association, formed with the express aim of welding into one body the whole militant proletariat of Europe and America, could not at once proclaim the principles laid down in the *Manifesto*. The International was bound to have a programme broad enough to be acceptable to the English trade unions, to the followers of Proudhon in France, Belgium, Italy, and Spain, and to the Lassalleans in Germany.*

Marx, who drew up this programme to the satisfaction of all parties, entirely trusted to the intellectual development of the working class, which was sure to result from combined action and mutual discussion. The very events and vicissitudes in the struggle against capital, the defeats even more than the victories, could not help bringing home to men's minds the insufficiency of their various favourite nostrums, and preparing the way for a more complete insight into the true conditions for working-class emancipation. And Marx was right. The International, on its breaking in 1874, left the workers quite different men from what it found them in 1864. Proudhonism in France, Lassalleanism in Germany, were dying out, and even the conservative English trade unions, though most of them had long since severed their connection with the International, were gradually advancing towards that point at which, last year at Swansea, their president could say in their name: 'Continental socialism has

* Lassalle personally, to us, always acknowledged himself to be a disciple of Marx, and, as such, stood on the ground of the *Manifesto*. But in his first public agitation, 1862–64, he did not go beyond demanding co-operative workshops supported by state credit.

lost its terror for us.' In fact, the principles of the *Manifesto* had made considerable headway among the working men of all countries.

The *Manifesto* itself came thus to the front again. Since 1850, the German text had been reprinted several times in Switzerland, England, and America. In 1872, it was translated into English in New York, where the translation was published in *Woorhull and Claflin's Weekly*. From this English version, a French one was made in *Le Socialiste* of New York. Since then, at least two more English translations, more or less mutilated, have been brought out in America, and one of them has been reprinted in England. The first Russian translation, made by Bakunin, was published at Herzen's Kolokol office in Geneva, about 1863; a second one, by the heroic Vera Zasulich, also in Geneva, in 1882. A new Danish edition is to be found in *Social-demokratisk Bibliothek*, Copenhagen, 1885; a fresh French translation in *Le Socialiste*, Paris, 1886. From this latter, a Spanish version was prepared and published in Madrid, 1886. The German reprints are not to be counted; there have been twelve altogether at the least. An Armenian translation, which was to be published in Constantinople some months ago, did not see the light, I am told, because the publisher was afraid of bringing out a book with the name of Marx on it, while the translator declined to call it his own production. Of further translations into other languages I have heard but had not seen. Thus the history of the *Manifesto* reflects the history of the modern working-class movement; at present, it is doubtless the most wide spread, the most international production of all socialist literature, the common platform acknowledged by millions of working men from Siberia to California.

Yet, when it was written, we could not have called it a *socialist* manifesto. By socialists, in 1847, were understood, on the one hand the adherents of the various utopian systems: Owenites in England, Fourierists in France, both of them already reduced to the position of mere sects, and gradually dying out; on the other hand, the most multifarious social quacks who, by all manner of tinkering, professed to redress, without any danger to capital and profit, all sorts of social grievances, in both cases men outside the working-class movement, and looking rather to the 'educated' classes for support. Whatever portion of the working class had become convinced of the insufficiency of mere political revolutions, and had proclaimed the necessity of total social change, called itself communist. It was a crude, rough-hewn, purely instinctive sort of communism; still, it touched the cardinal point and was powerful enough amongst the working class to produce the utopian communism of Cabet in France, and of Weitling in Germany. Thus, in 1847, socialism was a middle-class movement, communism a working-class movement. Socialism was, on the Continent at least, 'respectable'; communism was the very opposite. And as our notion, from the very beginning, was that 'the emancipation of the workers must be the act of the working class itself', there could be no doubt as to which of the two names we must take. Moreover, we have, ever since, been far from repudiating it.

The *Manifesto* being our joint production, I consider myself bound to state that the fundamental proposition which forms the nucleus belongs to Marx. That proposition is: That in every historical epoch, the prevailing mode of economic production and exchange, and the social organisation necessarily following from it, form the basis upon which it is built up, and from that which alone can be explained the political and intellectual history of that epoch; that consequently the whole history of mankind (since the dissolution of primitive tribal society, holding land in common ownership) has been a history of class struggles, contests between exploiting and exploited, ruling and oppressed classes; that the history of these class struggles forms a series of evolutions in which, nowadays, a stage has been reached where the exploited and oppressed class – the proletariat – cannot attain its emancipation from the sway of the exploiting and ruling class – the bourgeoisie – without, at the same time, and once and for all, emancipating society at large from all exploitation, oppression, class distinction, and class struggles.

This proposition, which, in my opinion, is destined to do for history what Darwin's theory has done for biology, we both of us, had been gradually approaching for some years before 1845. How far I had independently progressed towards it is best shown by my *Condition of the Working Class in England*. But when I again met Marx at Brussels, in spring 1845, he had it already worked out and put it before me in terms almost as clear as those in which I have stated it here.

From our joint preface to the German edition of 1872, I quote the following:

> However much that state of things may have altered during the last 25 years, the general principles laid down in the *Manifesto* are, on the whole, as correct today as ever. Here and there, some detail might be improved. The practical application of the principles will depend, as the *Manifesto* itself states, everywhere and at all times, on the historical conditions for the time being existing, and, for that reason, no special stress is laid on the revolutionary measures proposed at the end of Section II. That passage would, in many respects, be very differently worded today. In view of the gigantic strides of modern industry since 1848, and of the accompanying improved and extended organisation of the working class, in view of the practical experience gained, first in the February Revolution, and then, still more, in the Paris Commune, where the proletariat for the first time held political power for two whole months, this programme has in some details been antiquated. One thing especially was proved by the Commune, viz., that 'the working class cannot simply lay hold of ready-made state machinery, and wield

it for its own purposes'. (See *The Civil War in France: Address of the General Council of the International Working Men's Association, 1871*, where this point is further developed.) Further, it is self-evident that the criticism of socialist literature is deficient in relation to the present time, because it comes down only to 1847; also that the remarks on the relation of the communists to the various opposition parties (Section IV), although, in principle still correct, yet in practice are antiquated, because the political situation has been entirely changed, and the progress of history has swept from off the Earth the greater portion of the political parties there enumerated.

But then, the *Manifesto* has become a historical document which we have no longer any right to alter.

The present translation is by Mr Samuel Moore, the translator of the greater portion of Marx's *Capital*. We have revised it in common, and I have added a few notes explanatory of historical allusions.

Friedrich Engels
30 January 1888, London

The 1890 German Edition

Since [the 1883 German edition preface] was written, a new German edition of the *Manifesto* has again become necessary, and much has also happened to the manifesto which should be recorded here.

A second Russian translation – by Vera Zasulich – appeared in Geneva in 1882; the preface to that edition was written by Marx and myself. Unfortunately, the original German manuscript has gone astray; I must therefore retranslate from the Russian which will in no way improve the text. It reads:

[Reprint of the 1882 Russian Edition]

At about the same date, a new Polish version appeared in Geneva: *Manifest Kommunistyczny*.

Furthermore, a new Danish translation has appeared in the *Social-demokratisk Bibliothek*, Copenhagen, 1885. Unfortunately, it is not quite complete; certain essential passages, which seem to have presented difficulties to the translator, have been omitted, and, in addition, there are signs of carelessness here and there, which are all the more unpleasantly conspicuous since the translation indicates that had the translator taken a little more pains, he would have done an excellent piece of work.

A new French version appeared in 1886, in *Le Socialiste* of Paris; it is the best published to date.

From this latter, a Spanish version was published the same year in *El Socialista* of Madrid, and then reissued in pamphlet form: *Manifesto del Partido Communista* por Carlos Marx y F. Engels, Madrid, Administracion de El Socialista, Hernan Cortes.

As a matter of curiosity, I may mention that in 1887 the manuscript of an Armenian translation was offered to a publisher in Constantinople. But the good man did not have the courage to publish something bearing the name of Marx and suggested that the translator set down his own name as author, which the latter however declined.

After one, and then another, of the more or less inaccurate American translations had been repeatedly reprinted in England, an authentic version at last appeared in 1888. This was my friend Samuel Moore, and we went through it together once more before it went to press. It is entitled: *Manifesto of the Communist Party*, by Karl Marx and Frederick Engels. Authorised English translation, edited and annotated by Frederick Engels, 1888, London, William Reeves, 185 Fleet Street, E.C. I have added some of the notes of that edition to the present one.

The *Manifesto* has had a history of its own. Greeted with enthusiasm, at the time of its appearance, by the not at all numerous vanguard of scientific socialism (as is proved by the translations mentioned in the first place), it was soon forced into the background by the reaction that began with the defeat of the Paris workers in June 1848, and was finally excommunicated 'by law' in the conviction of the Cologne communists in November 1852. With the disappearance from the public scene of the workers' movement that had begun with the February Revolution, the *Manifesto* too passed into the background.

When the European workers had again gathered sufficient strength for a new onslaught upon the power of the ruling classes, the International Working

Men's Association came into being. Its aim was to weld together into one huge army the whole militant working class of Europe and America. Therefore it could not set out from the principles laid down in the *Manifesto*. It was bound to have a programme which would not shut the door on the English trade unions, the French, Belgian, Italian, and Spanish Proudhonists, and the German Lassalleans. This programme – the considerations underlying the statutes of the International – was drawn up by Marx with a master hand acknowledged even by Bakunin and the anarchists. For the ultimate final triumph of the ideas set forth in the *Manifesto*, Marx relied solely upon the intellectual development of the working class, as it necessarily has to ensue from united action and discussion. The events and vicissitudes in the struggle against capital, the defeats even more than the successes, could not but demonstrate to the fighters the inadequacy of their former universal panaceas, and make their minds more receptive to a thorough understanding of the true conditions for working-class emancipation. And Marx was right. The working class of 1874, at the dissolution of the International, was altogether different from that of 1864, at its foundation. Proudhonism in the Latin countries, and the specific Lassalleanism in Germany, were dying out; and even the ten arch-conservative English trade unions were gradually approaching the point where, in 1887, the chairman of their Swansea Congress could say in their name: 'Continental socialism has lost its terror for us.' Yet by 1887 continental socialism was almost exclusively the theory heralded in the *Manifesto*. Thus, to a certain extent, the history of the *Manifesto* reflects the history of the modern working-class movement since 1848. At present, it is doubtless the most widely circulated, the most international product of all socialist literature, the common programme of many millions of workers of all countries from Siberia to California.

Nevertheless, when it appeared, we could not have called it a *socialist* manifesto. In 1847, two kinds of people were considered socialists. On the one hand were the adherents of the various utopian systems, notably the Owenites in England and the Fourierists in France, both of whom, at that date, had already dwindled to mere sects gradually dying out. On the other, the manifold types of social quacks who wanted to eliminate social abuses through their various universal panaceas and all kinds of patch-work, without hurting capital and profit in the least. In both cases, people who stood outside the labour movement and who looked for support rather to the 'educated' classes. The section of the working class, however, which demanded a radical reconstruction of society, convinced that mere political revolutions were not enough, then called itself communist. It was still a rough-hewn, only instinctive and frequently somewhat crude communism. Yet, it was powerful enough to bring into being two systems of utopian communism – in France, the 'Icarian' communists of Cabet, and in Germany that of Weitling. Socialism in 1847 signified a bourgeois movement, communism a working-class movement. Socialism was, on the Continent at least, quite respectable, whereas communism was the very opposite. And since we were very decidedly of the opinion as early as then that 'the emancipation of the workers must be the task of the working class itself', we could have no hesitation as to which of the two names we should choose. Nor has it ever occurred to us to repudiate it.

'Working men of all countries, unite!' But few voices responded when we proclaimed these words to the world 42 years ago, on the eve of the first Paris Revolution in which the proletariat came out with the demands of its own. On 28 September 1864, however, the proletarians of most of the Western European countries joined hands in the International Working Men's Association of glorious memory. True, the International itself lived only nine years. But that the eternal union of the proletarians of all countries created by it is still alive and lives stronger than ever, there is no better witness than this day. Because today, as I write these lines, the European and American proletariat is reviewing its fighting forces, mobilised for the first time, mobilised as one army, under one flag, for one immediate aim: the standard eight-hour working day to be established by legal enactment, as proclaimed by the Geneva Congress of the International in 1866, and again by the Paris Workers' Congress of 1889. And today's spectacle will open the eyes of the capitalists and landlords of all countries to the fact that today the proletarians of all countries are united indeed.

If only Marx were still by my side to see this with his own eyes!

Friedrich Engels
1 May 1890, London

The 1892 Polish Edition

The fact that a new Polish edition of the *Communist Manifesto* has become necessary gives rise to various thoughts.

First of all, it is noteworthy that of late the *Manifesto* has become an index, as it were, of the development of large-scale industry on the European continent. In proportion as large-scale industry expands in a given country, the demand grows among the workers of that country for enlightenment regarding their position as the working class in relation to the possessing classes, the socialist movement spreads among them and the demand for the *Manifesto* increases. Thus, not only the state of the labour movement but also the degree of development of large-scale industry can be measured with fair accuracy in every country by the number of copies of the *Manifesto* circulated in the language of that country.

Accordingly, the new Polish edition indicates a decided progress of Polish industry. And there can be no doubt whatever that this progress since the previous edition published ten years ago has actually taken place. Russian Poland, Congress Poland, has become the big industrial region of the Russian Empire. Whereas Russian large-scale industry is scattered sporadically – a part round the Gulf of Finland, another in the centre (Moscow and Vladimir), a third along the coasts of the Black and Azov seas, and still others elsewhere – Polish industry has been packed into a relatively small area and enjoys both the advantages and disadvantages arising from such concentration. The competing Russian manufacturers acknowledged the advantages when they demanded protective tariffs against Poland, in spite of their ardent desire to transform the Poles into Russians. The disadvantages – for the Polish manufacturers and the Russian government – are manifest in the rapid spread of socialist ideas among the Polish workers and in the growing demand for the *Manifesto*.

But the rapid development of Polish industry, outstripping that of Russia, is in its turn a new proof of the inexhaustible vitality of the Polish people and a new guarantee of its impending national restoration. And the restoration of an independent and strong Poland is a matter which concerns not only the Poles but all of us. A sincere international collaboration of the European nations is possible only if each of these nations is fully autonomous in its own house.

The Revolution of 1848, which under the banner of the proletariat, after all, merely let the proletarian fighters do the work of the bourgeoisie, also secured the independence of Italy, Germany and Hungary through its testamentary executors, Louis Bonaparte and Bismarck; but Poland, which since 1792 had done more for the Revolution than all these three together, was left to its own resources when it succumbed in 1863 to a tenfold greater Russian force. The nobility could neither maintain nor regain Polish independence; today, to the bourgeoisie, this independence is, to say the least, immaterial. Nevertheless, it is a necessity for the harmonious collaboration of the European nations. It can be gained only by the young Polish proletariat, and in its hands it is secure. For the workers of all the rest of Europe need the independence of Poland just as much as the Polish workers themselves.

F. Engels
10 February 1892, London

The 1893 Italian Edition

Publication of the *Manifesto of the Communist Party* coincided, one may say, with 18 March 1848, the day of the revolution in Milan and Berlin, which were armed uprisings of the two nations situated in the centre, the one, of the continent of Europe, the other, of the Mediterranean; two nations until then enfeebled by division and internal strife, and thus fallen under foreign domination. While Italy was subject to the Emperor of Austria, Germany underwent the yoke, not less effective though more indirect, of the Tsar of all the Russias. The consequences of 18 March 1848 freed both Italy and Germany from this disgrace; if from 1848 to 1871 these two great nations were reconstituted and somehow again put on their own, it was as Karl Marx used to say, because the men who suppressed the Revolution of 1848 were, nevertheless, its testamentary executors in spite of themselves.

Everywhere that revolution was the work of the working class; it was the latter that built the barricades and paid with its lifeblood. Only the Paris workers, in overthrowing the government, had the very definite intention of overthrowing the bourgeois regime. But conscious though they were of the fatal antagonism existing between their own class and the bourgeoisie, still, neither the economic progress of the country nor the intellectual development of the mass of French workers had as yet reached the stage which would have made a social reconstruction possible. In the final analysis, therefore, the fruits of the revolution were reaped by the capitalist class. In the other countries, in Italy, in Germany, in Austria, the workers, from the very outset, did nothing but raise the bourgeoisie to power. But in any country the rule of the bourgeoisie is impossible without national independence. Therefore, the Revolution of 1848 had to bring in its train the unity and autonomy of the nations that had lacked them up to then: Italy, Germany, Hungary. Poland will follow in turn.

Thus, if the Revolution of 1848 was not a socialist revolution, it paved the way, prepared the ground for the latter. Through the impetus given to large-scaled industry in all countries, the bourgeois regime during the last 45 years has everywhere created a numerous, concentrated and powerful proletariat. It has thus raised, to use the language of the *Manifesto*, its own grave-diggers. Without restoring autonomy and unity to each nation, it will be impossible to achieve the international union of the proletariat, or the peaceful and intelligent co-operation of these nations toward common aims. Just imagine joint international action by the Italian, Hungarian, German, Polish and Russian workers under the political conditions preceding 1848!

The battles fought in 1848 were thus not fought in vain. Nor have the 45 years separating us from that revolutionary epoch passed to no purpose. The fruits are ripening, and all I wish is that the publication of this Italian translation may augur as well for the victory of the Italian proletariat as the publication of the original did for the international revolution.

The *Manifesto* does full justice to the revolutionary part played by capitalism in the past. The first capitalist nation was Italy. The close of the feudal Middle Ages, and the opening of the modern capitalist era are marked by a colossal figure: an Italian, Dante, both the last poet of the Middle Ages and the first poet of modern times. Today, as in 1300, a new historical era is approaching. Will Italy give us the new Dante, who will mark the hour of birth of this new, proletarian era?

Friedrich Engels
1 February 1893, London

4
AFTERWORD: INTRODUCTION TO THE 2008 EDITION

David Harvey

The *Communist Manifesto* of 1848 is an extraordinary document, full of insights, rich in meanings and bursting with political possibilities. Millions of people all around the world – peasants, workers, soldiers, intellectuals as well as professionals of all sorts – have, over the years, been touched and inspired by it. Not only did it render the dynamic political-economic world of capitalism more readily understandable, it moved millions from all walks of life to participate actively in the long, difficult and seemingly endless political struggle to alter the path of history, to make the world a better place through their collective endeavours. But why re-publish the *Manifesto* now? Does its rhetoric still work the old magic it once did? In what ways can this voice from the past speak to us now? Does its siren call to engage in class struggle still make sense?

While we may not have the right, as Marx and Engels wrote in their Preface to the 1872 edition, to alter what had even by then become a key historical document, we do have both the right and the political obligation to reflect upon and if necessary re-interpret its meanings, to interrogate its proposals, and, above all, to act upon the insights we derive from it. Of course, as Marx and Engels warn, 'the practical application of the principles will depend as the *Manifesto* itself states everywhere and at all times, on the historical' (and, I would add, geographical) 'conditions for the time-being existing'. We are certainly now, as of 2008, in the midst of one of those periodic commercial crises 'that put on trial', as the *Manifesto* notes, 'each time more threateningly, the existence of the entire bourgeois society'. And food riots are breaking out all over, particularly in many poorer nations, as food prices rise uncontrollably. So conditions seem propitious for a re-evaluation of the *Manifesto*'s relevance. Interestingly, one of its modest proposals for reform – the centralisation of credit in the hands of the state – seems to be well on the way to realisation, thanks to the collective actions of the US Federal Reserve, the European Central Bank and the central banks of the other leading capitalist powers in bailing out the world's financial system (the British ended up nationalising their leading ailing bank, Northern Rock). So why not take up some of the other equally modest but wholly sensible proposals – such as free (and good) education for all children in public schools; equal liability of all to labour; a heavy progressive or graduated income tax to rid ourselves of the appalling social and economic inequalities that now surround us? And maybe if we followed the proposal to curb the inheritance of personal wealth, then we might pay far more attention to the collective inheritance we pass on to our kids of a decent living and working environment as well as a natural world that maintains both its fecundity and charm.

So let us take this text, fashioned in the gloomy days of January 1848 in Brussels and focus its laser gaze upon on our own actually existing situation in London and Leeds, Los Angeles and New Orleans, Shanghai and Shenzhen, Buenos Aires and Cordoba, Johannesburg and Durban.... Here I am in a brilliantly lit New York City on 31 January 2008 – 160 years almost to the day after Marx put the final touches to the *Manifesto* – sitting down to write a new introduction to this well-thumbed text. I do so knowing that there are plenty of other past and present splendidly learned introductions available. But too many of the recent ones, in my judgement, view the *Manifesto* as a mere historical document whose time has passed, whose vision was either faulty or at least so deeply questionable as to make it irrelevant to our more complicated if not sophisticated times. The best we can do, when not cavilling at the text's obvious omissions and its equally obvious lapses with respect to what is now considered politically correct, is to admire the prose, annotate the references, trace the influences it encapsulated and projected, and bury the central political message either under a blanket of wistful leftist nostalgia or under a mass of academic footnotes. The collapse after 1989 of actually existing communisms and the conversion of those communist parties that do remain in power, as in China and West Bengal, into agents for a ruthlessly exploitative capitalism, have indeed cast a heavy pall over the political tradition that the *Manifesto* spawned. Who needs a communist manifesto after all of that burdened history?

But look around us and what do we see? Here in New York City the Wall Street bonuses have just been added up – a cool $33.2 billion (only a little less than the year before) for investment bankers who made a mess of the world's financial system and piled up financial losses now estimated to be at least $200 billion and daily mounting (some, like the International Monetary Fund, say it will be a trillion dollars lost before it is all over). When the bankers (with venerable names such as Merrill Lynch, Citicorp and the now defunct Bear Stearns) were first confronted with their difficulties in the summer of 2007, the world's central banks (led by the US Federal Reserve) rushed in with massive amounts of short-term credit and then cut interest rates to bail them out. Meanwhile at the source of the trouble lies a sub-prime mortgage crisis in the US in which close to 2 million people have already lost their homes to foreclosure (with many more in waiting) without any help forthcoming from anywhere (apart from a few tardy and largely symbolic gestures of support in Congress and a few band aids from financial institutions and understandably concerned local governments). The initial foreclosures were heavily concentrated among low-income African-Americans and women (particularly single-headed households) in the poorer sections of US cities where they leave a trail of boarded up and vandalised houses in totally devastated neighbourhoods. It begins to look as if a 'financial Katrina' has battered multiple cities around the USA. The society of 'the too much', of 'overproduction' and excessive speculation, has plainly broken down and reverted, as it always does, to 'a state of momentary barbarism'. Some of the corporate heads that innovated us into this mess have lost their jobs. But they had to pay nothing back of the many millions they earned in the halcyon years and some received incredibly generous golden handshakes when they stepped down – $161 million in the case of Stan O'Neal of Merrill Lynch and $40 million for Charles Prince of Citicorp (the head of the failed British bank Northern Rock departed with £750,000). Those foreclosed upon merely receive an extra tax bill, because forgiveness of a debt is assessed as income. And just to add insult to class injury, those companies and lawyers employed in the 'foreclosure mill', as it is now called, are reaping the handsomest of profits.

Who said class differences (neatly intertwined, as is all too often the case, with race and gender) are irrelevant to the sociality of our postmodern times?

This is what makes a contemporary reading of the *Manifesto* so astonishing, because the world the *Manifesto* describes has in no way disappeared. Do we not, after all, live in a world of turbocharged capitalism where greed, selfishness, competitive individualism and the lust for loot from any short-term gain at no matter whose or what else's expense surrounds us at every turn? Capitalism, Marx and Engels observe, 'cannot exist without perpetually revolutionising the instruments of production, and thereby the relations of production, and with them the whole relations of society' (including those of consumption). The resultant perpetual 'uninterrupted disturbance of social conditions', accompanied by 'everlasting uncertainty and agitation' generates incredible volatility in personal and local economic fortunes (to say nothing of endemic financial crises and dizzying gyrations in stock values). With wages 'ever more fluctuating' and livelihoods 'more and more precarious', personal insecurities (over jobs, social provision, pensions) and collective anxieties (over others who seem to threaten us) proliferate, militating against the civilised treatment of immigrants, dissidents and all those others who look or behave in a mode of difference. No wonder 'all that is solid' seems to be perpetually 'melting into air'. And does not the pervasive power and influence of corporate capital continue to strip 'of its halo every occupation' hitherto trusted to tell us the truth – 'the physician, the lawyer, the priest, the poet, the man of science' as well as the professors, pundits and media gurus to say nothing of all those bought politicians who do the bidding of moneyed interests? Is it not sad to note how much of what we call culture is 'a mere training to act as' (or attach oneself to) 'a machine' (or in our times an electronic device) and that the family, held up to us by sentimentalists as the solid rock of a civilised society, is 'reduced to a mere money relation', even when it is not mired in myriad hypocrisies? Do we not also feel more than a little alienated in a world where 'no other nexus between man and man' exists 'than naked self-interest, than callous cash payment', where people are viewed merely as objects and commodities in the market place, and where most of us work to create the wealth of others? What can we say about a world in which most labour has 'lost its charm' and relations of production have become merely 'despotic', and where all of us, from janitor to banker, are increasingly positioned as mere appendages to an ever-expanding and constantly accelerating capitalist accumulation machine that blindly continues on its path without the least concern for social or environmental consequences? Is it not perplexing that all of this is to be found in the midst of the greatest productive capacity, wondrous powers of transport and communications, and scientific-technical understandings that could surely be harnessed to permit a decent life and a safer future for all? And is it not, finally, deeply troubling to realise that the freedom and liberty promised again and again by the apologists and politicians mean nothing more than the freedom of the market and of market choice (dependent upon ability to pay) coupled with that 'single, unconscionable freedom – free trade'?

Communism may be declared dead, but a violent, brutalising, and perpetually revolutionising capitalism still flourishes. Marx and Engels in the *Manifesto* found a brilliant way to reveal to us what that capitalism was and is fundamentally about and how it came to be. In so doing they found an inspirational language with which not only to resist capitalism's class oppressions and penchant for creative destruction, but also to illuminate the way to transform capitalism, with all of its remarkable achievements (achievements that Marx and Engels freely acknowledged in their own time as we must surely do, even more so, in ours), into something radically different and far more humane. Given the class character of this monstrous system, they also took the clear, logical and obvious step of insisting that the only way to engage in this transformative project was to wage a politics of class struggle. To the degree that the circumstances of their dystopian account have been ameliorated over the years, and the conditions they describe do not fully pertain, then it is to the grand history of popular resistance and class struggle since 1848 that we must bend a knee.

Imagine, furthermore, the shock of recognition with which the laid-off steelworkers in Pittsburgh, Sheffield and Essen, or the once solidly employed textile workers in the mills of Manchester, Mumbai, Mulhouse and South Carolina, would read the following passage:

> All old-established national industries have been destroyed or are daily being destroyed. They are dislodged by new industries, whose introduction becomes a life and death question for all civilised nations, by industries that no longer work up indigenous raw material, but raw material drawn from the remotest zones; industries whose products are consumed, not only at home, but in every quarter of the globe. In place of the old wants, satisfied by the production of the country, we find new wants, requiring for their satisfaction the products of distant lands and climes. In place of the old local and national seclusion and self-sufficiency, we have intercourse in every direction, universal inter-dependence of nations....
>
> The bourgeoisie, by the rapid improvement of all instruments of production, by the immensely facilitated means of communication, draws all, even the most barbarian, nations into civilisation. The cheap prices of commodities are the heavy artillery with which it batters down all Chinese walls, with which it forces the barbarians' intensely obstinate hatred of foreigners to capitulate. It compels all nations, on pain of extinction, to adopt the bourgeois mode of production; it compels them to introduce what it calls civilisation into their midst, i.e., to become bourgeois themselves. In one word, it creates a world after its own image.

Nowadays, of course, it is goods from China that are battering down our walls, as we go off to shop in the Wal-Mart store (where 'Made in China' predominates) to seek satisfaction for all those new wants for products drawn from distant lands and climes. The *Manifesto*'s prescient description of what we now call globalisation (with its cognates of off-shoring and de-industrialisation and global interdependence) suggests a certain continuity within the historical geography of capitalism from 1848 until today. Meanwhile nation states, facing an increasing centralisation of corporate capitalist power and expanding populations, become even more enmeshed in capitalist rules of the game through international agreements like the World Trade Organisation, NAFTA and the European Union, backed up by powerful international institutions (such as the International Monetary Fund). These forces all connive at the breaking down of trade barriers while consolidating a rule of law in which the rights of private property and the profit rate trump all other forms of human right you can think of. Competition between states and industrial regions (Bavaria, Silicon Valley, the Pearl River delta, Bangalore) re-enforces this capitalist logic of exploitation and imprints capitalist, and in these times distinctively neoliberal, values ever deeper in our psyches. Failing all this, the powers of the leading imperialist states are deployed to violently inflict the corporate agenda (check out the constitution imposed on Iraq in the first phases of US occupation) upon the world. And lest we think such violence is new or idiosyncratic to George W. Bush and his now not-so-merry crew of disgraced neoconservative theorists, consider what that archetypal liberal President Wilson of the United States had to say in 1919:

> 'Since trade ignores national boundaries and the manufacturer insists on having the world as a market, the flag of his nation must follow him, and the doors of the nations which are closed against him must be battered down. Concessions obtained by financiers must be safeguarded by ministers of state, even if the sovereignty of unwilling nations be outraged in the process. Colonies must be obtained or planted, in order that no useful corner of the world may be overlooked or left unused.'[1]

How far capitalism had advanced down the path of globalisation and construction of the world market by 1848 was, of course, miniscule compared to the enormous strides made since then. So how was it that Marx and Engels could produce such a prophetic document? All too aware of the storm clouds of capitalist crisis and social revolution then gathering across Europe, they were charged with writing a manifesto for a pan-European and mainly clandestine movement of those who called themselves communists. Since nobody at that time had any clear idea of what communism might mean, the door was open for a creative shot at defining the nascent movement's mission. Marx's critical studies of political economy (mainly British) and of the revelatory writings of the utopian socialists (mainly French though Robert Owen was also important) had alerted him to the nature of the fundamental driving forces behind capitalist development, and this, coupled with Engels' first-hand knowledge of Manchester industrialism (set out in 1844 in *The Condition of the Working Classes in England*), allowed them both to glimpse a vision of what the world would be like if it all became like Manchester, as it surely would if there were no resistance.

Marx (for it was he who, by Engels' account, did the final writing) produced a brilliant synthesis of insights, a succinct description, in immediately recognisable and the simplest of terms, of what capitalism was and still is fundamentally about, where it had come from, what its potentialities were, and where it was likely to go to in the absence of coherent opposition on the part of those who created the wealth, the working classes. Go now to the Pearl River delta (with factories employing as many as 40,000 workers), the maquila zones of Mexico, the clothing factories in Bangladesh, the sewing shops of the Philippines, the shoe producers in Vietnam, the mines of Brazil and Orissa, and dare to say they were wrong!! Two billion proletarians have been added to the global wage labour force over the last 20 years – the opening of China, the collapse of the erstwhile Communist Bloc and the incorporation of formerly independent peasant populations in India and Indonesia as well as throughout Latin America and Africa playing a crucial role. A no-holds-barred corporate capitalism has re-emerged over the last 30 years to take advantage of this situation. In China, Bangladesh, Indonesia, Guatemala and Vietnam, contemporary descriptions of the catastrophic conditions of labouring could be inserted into Marx's chapter on 'the Working Day' in *Capital* without anyone being able to tell the difference. And the most rabid forms of exploitation rest, as is so often the case, on the backs of women and people of colour. Meanwhile, in the advanced capitalist countries, those who once had proud positions as unionised workers in powerful industries find themselves living in the midst of the wreckage of processes of deindustrialisation that have destroyed whole communities and left cities like Detroit, Baltimore, Sheffield and Essen, as well as a once thriving textile industry in Mumbai, a legacy of empty factories and warehouses awaiting hopeful conversion into condominiums, casinos or shopping malls with perhaps a museum of industrial history to house memories, both brutal and triumphant, of the class war once waged with that particular form of industrial capitalism.

So what do we make today of the obvious inference that the only way to resist these depredations is to wage class struggle and that to do so workers of the world must unite? 'Class struggle' is, admittedly, a blanket term that conceals myriad variations. To simply parrot the phrase without doing the requisite analysis as to exactly what it means in different places and times is to disrespect the analytic tradition of historical materialism that Marx and Engels bequeathed us. Classes are always in the process of formation and re-formation and while on the one hand Marx and Engels thought they detected a tendency towards a grand polarisation between bourgeoisie and proletariat emerging, they also recognised forces of fragmentation and slow dissolution of past class forms. Western Marxists these days, of course, are wont to complain that the working class has disappeared. But what has simply happened is that technological changes, the shift towards a service economy and widespread deindustrialisation have seriously weakened traditional working-class institutions in those countries where Western Marxists dwell, while massive processes of proletarianisation have gone on elsewhere. For our times, therefore, it becomes necessary to pay attention to those processes of class formation and re-formation occurring with such dramatic force in China, Indonesia, India, Vietnam, the ex-Soviet Bloc as well as throughout Latin America, the Middle East and Africa. Nor should we presume these days, if we ever should have, that class formation is confined within nation states, since cross-border and even transnational relations among workers moving within migration streams and forming diasporas are every bit as intricate as those to be found within a capitalist class that many now regard as being almost by definition transnational. These are the sorts of situations and processes we need to analyse with the greatest care if we are to accurately gauge the economic situation and calculate the political possibilities of our time.

Marx and Engels also liked to argue that the working classes could (or should?) claim no country since they had long been deprived of access to and control over the means of production. But even in their time, as they recognised towards the end of the *Manifesto*, national differences clearly mattered. They recognised that uneven geographical development of both bourgeois and working-class power were creating different conditions of political struggle in, for example, England, France, Poland, Switzerland and Germany. And so it is today. Nations are pitted against nations, regions against regions, cities against cities, if only in the competitive struggle to attract investment, and workers, desperate for jobs, are corralled into supporting local alliances to promote development packages and projects that offer sweet subsidies to highly mobile multinational capital to come to or stay in town. And to the degree that capitalists can distract attention from their own perfidious role in the ruthless exploitation of labour power in the workshops of production, by blaming immigrants, foreign competition and the 'uncivilised' habits of despised others for all the problems that local workers face, so the prospective unity of the working classes is rendered far more difficult. The divide and rule tactics of exploiting not only national but also ethnic, gender and religious differences within the working classes take an inevitable toll and all too often end up fomenting and even entrenching a politics of exclusions rather than of incorporation into a global dynamic of class struggle.

Furthermore, as the example of the Wall Street bonuses and the home foreclosures with which I began demonstrates, the field of class struggle stretches way beyond the factory and into the nether corners of everyone's daily lives. The class violence (articulated through racism and sexism) entailed in the foreclosure wave could not be clearer. As the *Manifesto* concedes, workers, having hopefully earned a living wage, are then 'set upon by other portions of the bourgeoisie, the landlord, the shopkeeper, the pawnbroker' and, we should add, the masters of credit, for yet another round of exploitation. Predatory activities of this sort played, however, a primary role in the historical emergence of capitalism. It was the merchant capitalists who robbed much of the world not only of silver and precious metals but also of the products of labour produced under all manner of other social conditions in 'distant lands and climes'. It was the usurers who helped undermine feudal power and thereby release a huge army of retainers into the wage labour force. This 'primitive accumulation' did not stop, however, with the rise of industrial capitalism. The depredations of imperialism, colonialism and neo-colonialism continue to this day to rob much of the rest of the world of value, of cultural and natural resources in order to support the ever-escalating affluence of the capitalist classes, particularly in the core regions of global capitalism (though now countries like Mexico, China, Russia and India have their aliquot share of billionaires). Not content with robbery in the nether regions of the world, corporate capitalists and financiers, as the foreclosure example demonstrates, are all too willing to cannibalise wealth from within their own territories (just look at what has been happening as workers lose not only their houses but also their hard-won pension and healthcare rights in the US and Europe). These on-going predatory practices of what I call 'accumulation by dispossession' are everywhere apparent and spark an enormous variety of struggles against the loss of assets here, environmental and resource degradations there and outright thievery, fraud and violent robbery somewhere else.[2]

While the differences and varieties of struggle are palpable, we must perforce recognise, Marx and Engels insist, the commonalities underlying our diverse fates and fortunes. It is crucial that we become politically aware as to the fundamental nature of capitalism and the possibilities for transformation latent within it. This is the political task that the *Manifesto* so cogently addresses. And if Marx and Engels return to the proletariat again and again as the central agent of radical and transformative change it is for two very specific analytic reasons that hold as powerfully true today as they did in 1848. The first lies in the simple fact that the profit that capitalists perpetually seek ultimately rests on the production of a surplus product and of surplus value (profit) through the exploitation of living labour in the act of production. But by virtue of this pivotal position, workers also have the potential power to bring the capitalist system to a halt and thereby radically transform it because it is their labour and their labour alone that powers the system onwards.

To be sure, there are all sorts of other struggles going on around us that distract attention from this central point of struggle. There is persistent tension within the capitalist class as to how the surplus might be distributed, for example, between financiers, merchants, industrialists, landlords, service providers, the state, and the like. From time to time major reforms have to be instituted to curb the excesses of this or that faction (e.g. the financiers in the present conjuncture clearly need to be reined in by regulation). And there are similar struggles between factions within the working classes, pitting industrial, agricultural, service and state employees against each other, to say nothing of the fomented nationalist and ethnic differences that pit, for example, US against Chinese workers in the desperate search to procure and protect jobs. Geo-economic and geopolitical conflicts between the different geographical regions of capital accumulation (everything from inter-urban competition to regional class alliances and transnational groupings such as the European Union, East Asia, NAFTA and Mercosur) also periodically erupt to obscure other dimensions of struggle. But at the end of the day, Marx and Engels logically conclude, the only form of class struggle that can radically change the system is one that is led by all those who produce the wealth of others in general and the capitalist class in particular, and that is defined as the proletariat.

This then poses a difficult organisational question: how can all these proletarians located all around the world and working under the most disparate of circumstances come together to change the world? On this point the *Manifesto* has some interesting ideas. Struggle, Marx and Engels suggest, begins with the alienated individual who understands precisely how, to cite the slogan made famous by contemporary feminists, the personal is political. Passivity in the face of thievery, domination and exploitation is no option. Assembled together in factories, fields, offices and institutions, individuals come together and develop a collective understanding of the common sources of their discontents and frustrations. From this they begin to sense the class identity implicit in their varied experiences and on that common basis start to articulate collective arguments and demands. And as they build collective organisations to agitate for satisfaction of their wants, needs and creative desires, they construct territorial groupings – in neighbourhoods, cities, metropolitan regions – within and from which a broader political and cultural commonality arises. This new sociality, when linked together with other distinctive regions by the ever-more sophisticated means of transport and communications that capitalism constructs to facilitate commodity exchange and the circulation of capital, opens up the prospect to conquer the nation state as a dominant container of power. But political agitation cannot stop at that geographical scale either, for only when workers of the world can unite around a common vision (albeit one that rests on enormous differences) can capitalism be tamed and the communist vision of an alternative come to fruition. The organisational form of the class struggle has to be prepared, in short, to 'jump geographical scales' and move smoothly from the local to the global and back again.

The history of communist movements demonstrates all too tragically what happens when the movement forgets that these different moments and geographical scales of political struggle are dialectically integrated and mutually constitutive of each other. If the way the personal is political fails to build towards an open dynamics of regional cultural consciousness formation, then the organisational schema proposed in the *Manifesto* fails. Even more importantly, if the actions taken in the name of the nation state, once captured by proletarian powers, do not resolve the alienations and frustrations of individuals, then the local and regional organisational forms painstakingly and lovingly built in a spirit of revolutionary hope become hollowed out, static and unresponsive bureaucratic shells. The necessity for both progressive and permanent revolutions (of the sort that capitalism so successfully and vigorously prosecutes through its own dynamism) cannot be neglected. Failing this, the revolutionary movement relapses into stasis (as it did in the ex-Soviet Union) and becomes an all-too easy target for capitalist counter-revolution. The dialectics of organisational form outlined in the *Manifesto* require careful elaboration and application if the revolutionary movement is to succeed.

But there is a further lesson to be learned from the *Manifesto*'s form of analysis. Consider, for example, how the bourgeoisie came to power. Merchant capital went outside of the constraints of feudal power in its explorations and exploitation of the world market. In effect this was a geographical strategy that gained power from outside of the bastions of feudalism and then, having surrounded the latter, forced them to surrender to bourgeois power. The state that protected feudal interests was captured and transformed and put to bourgeois uses (is the US state as currently constituted anything other than an executive committee for the protection of corporate interests?). The lesson for any revolutionary movement is that the territorialisation of political struggle, the occupation of this or that region or nation state as a staging ground for broader assaults upon the political power of capitalist elites, is important. While socialism in one country (let alone city) may be impossible, this does not mean that the territorialisation of political struggle, the occupation of this or that city, region or nation state as a staging ground for broader assaults upon the political power of capitalist elites, is irrelevant. But there were many other elements in the situation that permitted the bourgeois rise to power – the existence of a landless labour force, a rising market demand, an influx of money and gold – and it was into this situation that those armed with a certain money power could step and position themselves as full-fledged capitalists. As Marx notes elsewhere, radical social transformations such as the rise of capitalism or the transition to communism, do not occur in empty space but depend crucially on the prior construction of the conditions that make such transformations possible. While Marx and Engels do not go on to make the point specifically, the advantages Britain possessed in all these respects undoubtedly played a crucial role in explaining why a nascent capitalism everywhere could most easily take root in that particular part of the world from the sixteenth century onwards. Furthermore, capitalists when hit with crises of overproduction and over-accumulation, as they inevitably are, once again 'go geographical' in expanding their geographical range of market and investment possibilities. This tendency to look for what I call 'a spatial fix' to problems of overproduction has played an incredibly important role in the perpetuation of the globalisation processes that Marx and Engels so succinctly described in 1848.[3]

The implication is that communism has to emerge from within the nexus of possibilities that capitalism inevitably creates. It has to be alert to those moves that the bourgeoisie makes to deal with the crises it foments – such as the current moves to centralise credit in the hands of the state apparatuses in order to control the financial crisis – and treat these moves as political opportunities to seize hold of new powers and to define new trajectories of social change. Furthermore, communism has to take root in those regions where the conditions are most favourable for its development. It then has to pursue a territorial and geographical strategy to surround and undermine the central loci of capitalist power. Unfortunately, in the class struggles that have been waged across the world these last 200 years, capitalists have again and again used their superior command over space as a way to beat down revolutionary movements in particular places (Chile, Portugal and Mozambique in the 1970s come immediately to mind). Workers of the world must not only unite to pursue their revolutionary claims: they must also devise sophisticated political and geopolitical strategies to win the right to construct a different kind of world order.

But to what, exactly, should the workers' movement lay claim? Let us look more closely at what capitalists actually do. They begin the day with a certain amount of money, they go into the market place and buy labour power and means of production, they select (purchase) a technology, set these all to work to produce a new commodity and then sell that commodity for the original money plus a profit (a surplus value). The next day they wake up and have to decide what to do with the surplus money they gained the day before. They face a Faustian dilemma: reinvest to get even more money or consume their surplus away in pleasures. The coercive laws of competition force them to reinvest because if one does not reinvest then another surely will. To remain a capitalist, some surplus must be reinvested to make even more surplus. Successful capitalists usually make more than enough surplus to reinvest in expansion and satisfy their desire for pleasure. But the result of perpetual reinvestment is the expansion of surplus production at a compound rate – hence all the logistical growth curves (money, capital, output and population) that attach to the history of capital accumulation.

The politics of capitalism are affected by the perpetual need to find profitable terrains for capital surplus production and absorption. In this the capitalist faces a number of obstacles to continuous and trouble-free expansion. If there is a scarcity of labour and wages are too high then either existing labour has to be disciplined (technologically induced unemployment or an assault on organised working class power – such as that set in motion by Thatcher and Reagan in the 1980s – are two prime methods) or fresh labour forces must be found (by immigration, export of capital or proletarianisation of hitherto independent elements in the population). New means of production in general and new natural resources in particular must be found. This puts increasing pressure on the natural environment to yield up the necessary raw materials and absorb the inevitable wastes. The coercive laws of competition also force new technologies and organisational forms to come on line all the time, since capitalists with higher productivity can out-compete those using inferior methods. The perpetual revolutions in technologies that the *Manifesto* describes are destabilising to the point where they can threaten profitability. Innovations also define new wants and needs, reduce the turnover time of capital and the friction of distance. This last effect extends the geographical range over which the capitalist is free to search for expanded labour supplies and raw materials. If there is not enough purchasing power in the market then new markets must be found by expanding foreign trade, promoting new products and lifestyles, creating new credit instruments and debt-financed state and personal expenditures. If, finally, the profit rate is too low, then state regulation of 'ruinous competition', monopolisation (mergers and acquisitions) and capital exports to fresh pastures provide ways out.

If any one of the above barriers to continuous capital circulation and expansion becomes impossible to circumvent, then capital accumulation is blocked and capitalists face a crisis: capital cannot be profitably re-invested, accumulation stagnates or ceases and capital is devalued (lost) and in some instances even physically destroyed. Failure to negotiate the labour barrier produces a profit squeeze crisis because higher wages cut into profits; the failure to find ways to negotiate natural resource and waste disposal barriers produces environmental crises (sometimes referred to as 'the second contradiction of capitalism'); rapid technological changes produce a falling rate of profit problem; lack of (usually credit-fuelled) effective demand generates a crisis of underconsumption. There is no singular theory of crisis formation within capitalism, just a series of barriers that throw up multiple possibilities for different kinds of crises. At one particular historical moment conditions may lead to one kind of crisis dominating, but on other occasions several forms can combine and on still others the crisis tendencies get displaced spatially (into geopolitical and geo-economic crises) or temporally (as financial crises). The effect, however, is always one of the devaluation of capital. Devaluation can take a number of forms. Surplus commodities can be devalued or destroyed, productive capacity and the assets can be written down in value and left unemployed, or money itself can be devalued through inflation. And in a major crisis, of course, labour stands to be devalued through massive unemployment.

Once the barriers are circumvented or dissolve, accumulation typically revives at its compound rate. We have come to accept unthinkingly that a healthy economy grows and that growth is therefore normal and good, no matter what the social, political or environmental consequences. But it boggles the mind to imagine what the world will be like after another hundred years of compound growth at, say, 2–3 per cent per year. Plainly, some other way must be found to organise the social order if humanity is to survive.

So what, then, should a revolutionary movement demand? The answer is simple enough in principle: greater collective and democratic control over what is produced, how and by whom as well as strong command over the use of whatever surpluses are produced. To have a surplus product is not a bad thing: indeed, in many situations a surplus is crucial to adequate survival and it is only with an adequate surplus that many of the good things in life can be provided (cities, for example, could not exist without the mobilisation and concentration of a surplus product). Throughout capitalist history, some of the surplus value created has been taxed away by the state and in social democratic phases that proportion rose significantly putting much of the surplus under state control. At least some of it went to purposes (such as universal healthcare, social housing and education) that benefited hitherto oppressed, marginalised and excluded populations. The whole neoliberal project over the last 30 years has been oriented towards rolling back those benefits and establishing private control over the use of the surplus. The data for all OECD countries show, however, that the share of gross output taken by the state has been roughly constant since the 1970s. The main achievement of the neoliberal assault, then, has been to prevent the state share expanding in the way it did in the 1950s and 1960s in the leading capitalist countries (even including the United States). One further response on the part of the capitalist class has been to create new systems of governance that integrate state and corporate interests and, through the application of money power, assure that control over the disbursement of the surplus through the state apparatus favours corporate capital (like Halliburton and the pharmaceutical companies) and the upper classes. Increasing the share of the surplus under state control will only work if the state apparatus itself is brought back under collective democratic control.

How the surplus is distributed and used is only one of the several pressing political issues for our times. We live on a planet of burgeoning slums, sites of teeming human possibilities and innovative activities in the midst of total degradation, violence, criminality and despair, alongside a rising tide of unconstrained and in some instances criminally profligate consumerism that seemingly knows no bounds. The astonishing inequalities that now exist clearly need to be rectified. But the fragmentations encountered make it more and more difficult to imagine a collective politics of hope let alone a well-organised class struggle. In the rapidly urbanising developing world in particular, the city

> 'is splitting into different separated parts, with the apparent formation of many "microstates". Wealthy neighborhoods provided with all kinds of services, such as exclusive schools, golf courses, tennis courts and private police patrolling the area around the clock intertwine with illegal settlements where water is available only at public fountains, no sanitation system exists, electricity is pirated by a privileged few, the roads become mud streams whenever it rains, and where house-sharing is the norm. Each fragment appears to live and function autonomously, sticking firmly to what it has been able to grab in the daily fight for survival.'[4]

But important though the politics of redistribution of wealth may be, it is, in Marx and Engels' judgement, far too limiting as a political project. What distinguishes distributive socialism from communism is that the communists focus on the organisation and politics of production in general via a critique of the manner of capitalist production of surplus value and surplus product in particular. In Marx and Engels' time, simple acquaintance with what life was like in the factories, fields and workshops of the world, as well as in the living spaces of an inadequately remunerated working class, was enough to provoke the outrage of the bourgeois factory and public health inspectors as well as the general public once these conditions were revealed for all to see. And this is the fundamental condition that communists seek to change. Those who controlled and used the means of production and used them for their own exclusive benefit were plainly at fault and it was therefore the mission of the communist movement to eradicate that class privilege and organise production through the association of workers backed by democratic control of the state apparatus (this is as far as the *Manifesto* goes). We now know that such a general alternative plan was not and is not so easy to devise and implement. But the conditions of labouring and living in much of the world are now in such a parlous state as to suggest that the communist imperative to revolutionise the organisation of production and consumption on non-capitalist lines is more crucial now than it ever was in 1848. But to this there is now an added urgency. The compound rates of growth implied by the capitalist requirement to produce surplus value *ad infinitum* via the production of a surplus product, are daily growing more threatening to planetary ecosystems and to the provision of basic requirements for energy, water and clean air. The compounding rates of capitalist growth cannot last for ever and something new – a steady state economy, for example, which would be totally incompatible with capitalism – has to be devised and that will require, whether we regard ourselves as communists or not, addressing the fundamental question of how to organise both production and consumption on more rational, equitable and sane lines. The warning signs of trouble in the bourgeois construction of paradise are all around us. Even a casual reading of them surely suggests that Marx and Engels were right to stress then as we should even more so now, that it is high time for capitalism to be gone, to make way for some superior mode of production.

It is imperative, therefore, that we re-ignite the political passions that suffuse *The Communist Manifesto*. Communists, Marx and Engels aver, have no political party. They simply constitute themselves at all times and in all places as those who understand the limits, failings and destructive tendencies of the capitalist order as well as the innumerable ideological masks and false legitimations that capitalists and their apologists produce in order to perpetuate their singular class power. Communists are all those who work incessantly to produce a different future to that which capitalism portends. While institutionalised communism may be dead, there are by this measure millions of communists among us, willing to act upon their understandings, ready to creatively pursue to the political imperatives that the *Manifesto* defines, and, above all, ready to open their hearts and minds to this inspirational message that echoes down to us from the doleful days of 1848. We communists are the persistent spectral presence, conjured up by the bourgeoisie out of the nether world, the sorcerers who can weave our own distinctive magic, our own sense of class destiny, into the woof and weft of our historical geography. 'Change the world', said Marx: 'Change Life', said Rimbaud; 'for us', said André Breton, 'these two projects are the same'. The struggle continues.

Acknowledgement

I thank Fernando Coronil for perceptive comments on an early draft.

Notes

1. Cited in N. Chomsky, *On Power and Ideology*, Boston, South End Press, 1990, p. 14.
2. D. Harvey, *A Brief History of Neoliberalism*, Oxford, Oxford University Press, 2005.
3. D. Harvey, *Spaces of Global Capitalism: Towards a Theory of Uneven Geographical Development*, London, Verso, 2006.
4. M. Balbo cited in National Research Council, *Cities Transformed: Demographic Change and Its Implications in the Developing World*, Washington, DC, The National Academies Press, 2003, p. 379; M. Davis, *Planet of Slums*, London, Verso, 2006.

Karl Marx was born in 1818. In 1848 he collaborated with Friedrich Engels in writing *The Communist Manifesto*. Expelled from Prussia in the same year, Marx took up residence first in Paris and then in London where, in 1867, he published his magnum opus *Capital*. A co-founder of the International Workingmen's Association in 1864, Marx died in London in 1883.

Friedrich Engels was born in 1820. He moved to England in 1842 to work in his father's Manchester textile firm. After joining the fight against the counter-revolution in Germany in 1848 he returned to Manchester and the family business. In subsequent years he provided financial support for Marx and edited the second and third volumes of *Capital*. He died in 1895.

Jodi Dean is a political philosopher and professor in the Political Science department at Hobart and William Smith Colleges. Her most recent books include *The Communist Horizon* (Verso, 2012) and *Crowds and Party* (Verso, 2016).

David Harvey is Distinguished Professor of Anthropology at the Graduate Centre of the City University of New York. His recent books include *Seventeen Contradictions and the End of Capitalism* (Profile Books, 2014) and *The Ways of the World* (Profile Books, 2016).